ACTIVITIES, GAMES, and LESSONS for SOCIAL LEARNING

For my students, for all you have taught me.

—Julie A. Erdelyi

To all educators who seek knowledge about
research-informed practices so all learners succeed.

—Blanche Podhajski

ACTIVITIES, GAMES, and LESSONS for SOCIAL LEARNING

A PRACTICAL GUIDE

Julie Erdelyi for

Stern Center
for Language and Learning

Foreword by Kari Dunn Buron

FOR INFORMATION:

Corwin

A SAGE Company

2455 Teller Road

Thousand Oaks, California 91320

(800) 233-9936

www.corwin.com

SAGE Publications Ltd.

1 Oliver's Yard

55 City Road

London EC1Y 1SP

United Kingdom

SAGE Publications India Pvt. Ltd.

B 1/I 1 Mohan Cooperative Industrial Area

Mathura Road, New Delhi 110 044

India

SAGE Publications Asia-Pacific Pte. Ltd.

18 Cross Street #10-10/11/12

China Square Central

Singapore 048423

Printed in the United States of America

ISBN 978-1-5443-6245-8

Program Director: Jessica Allan

Senior Content Development Editor: Lucas Schleicher

Associate Content Development Editor: Mia Rodriguez

Production Editor: Amy Schroller

Copy Editor: Karin Rathert

Typesetter: C&M Digitals (P) Ltd.

Proofreader: Susan Schon

Indexer: Sheila Hill

Cover Designer: Rose Storey

Marketing Manager: Deena Meyer

This book is printed on acid-free paper.

20 21 22 23 24 10 9 8 7 6 5 4 3 2 1

Contents

Section I: Teaching Self-Regulation

CHAPTER ONE

CHAPTER TWO

Section 2: Teaching Social Communication

Section 3: Teaching Perspective-Taking

CONCLUSION

Visit the companion website at
resources.corwin.com/ActivitiesGamesLessons
for downloadable resources.

List of Tables and Figures

*Figures listed with an asterisk are available as full-sized templates in the Resources section, beginning on page 125.

Foreword

The importance of teaching social and emotional skills to develop emotional intelligence cannot be understated. Emotional intelligence refers to how well one handles oneself across all life environments, and research has demonstrated that direct and systematic teaching of such skills not only increases prosocial behavior but also increases academic performance.

Children who struggle with social cognitive delays and problems of emotion regulation often demonstrate challenging behaviors when faced with the highly social environment of school. Behaviors such as aggression, verbal outbursts, and self-aggression can be related to a person's inability to manage emotions or even understand the emotional responses of others. When individuals don't have effective emotion regulation skills, they might become dysfunctional in their ability to successfully negotiate common situations that elicit large emotions. In his book *The Brain and Emotional Intelligence* (2011), Daniel Goleman cited the following skill areas as necessary for one individual to have a positive impact on another: self-awareness, social awareness, self-management, and relationship management. In her new book, *Activities, Games and Lessons for Social Learning*, Julie Erdelyi directly addresses these crucial cognitive areas of concern through game play. The book serves as a "how to" manual for using common games to practice the cognitive skills necessary to understand another person's perspective, regulate one's own emotions, and communicate effectively with others.

Julie Erdelyi has worked in special education for 20 years in direct service, program management, and consultation and as such, is uniquely qualified to write about her experiences with social teaching. Julie has specialized in working with students who struggle with issues of self-regulation, social communication, and perspective-taking and she has addressed all three of these cognitive areas in her book.

Typical children learn social and emotional information through thousands of hours of social interaction. Children who are delayed in their development of the skills needed to effectively interact, make friends, and socially succeed, do not have thousands of opportunities to practice and learn these skills. Therefore, it is essential to teach social and emotional skills directly and in a highly systematic way. It is also essential that teachers address the generalization of such skills once they are learned.

Erdelyi's manual is organized with sections addressing self-regulation, social communication, and perspective-taking. Each section introduces common games that can be used to practice those social cognitive skills. Each section clearly states what skill is being practiced with each game, why it is important to practice that skill, and how to teach students to generalize the skill meaningfully into their life. This book is relevant and valuable to all teachers who struggle to support their most difficult students.

—**Kari Dunn Buron**
Autism Education Specialist/Author
www.5pointscale.com

Preface

Over the years, as I began teaching teachers in addition to my school-aged students, I noticed trends in the questions that teachers were asking: *Why are kids entering school coming to us with fewer established social skills? Why are we seeing an increase in children who are struggling with self-regulation?* Many of the answers to these questions are yet to be discovered. Our society is experiencing an explosion in the development and use of technology and an evolution of family systems and trends in parenting, social structures, and economic disparities. My teachers wanted to know what they can do to be more effective in their jobs and in helping children. Overwhelmingly, the answer that works for them is incorporating social emotional learning into their classrooms.

It turns out, the teachers are right. Providing social emotional learning in schools has many positive impacts for students. In a meta-analysis conducted by Durlak, Weissberg, Dymnicki, Taylor, and Schellinger (2011) involving 270,034 K–12 students, those who participated in social emotional learning demonstrated academic achievement that reflected an 11 percent gain over those who did not. Students who participated in social emotional learning programs showed improved social and emotional skills, attitudes, and behaviors.

It takes time, training, and practice to adjust to teaching any new subject, and this includes social emotional learning. Teachers have tight schedules and many demands on their time. Finding the time to incorporate social learning into a typical classroom day may seem challenging. Teachers taking my courses have expressed the need to teach social learning skills and also the need to have some ready-to-go resources to do this. They often ask, "Do you have materials to share with us?" and, "Is this lesson written down, and can you share it?" I will surely continue my practice of sharing my lessons and materials as I develop them, but they have made the message clear: Write a manual.

WHO IS THIS BOOK FOR?

While teachers are the audience who inspired this book, it became readily apparent that others might also find it interesting and useful. Special educators, speech pathologists, social workers, therapists, and parents can use this book to provide explicit social emotional teaching. Please note that the use of the word "teacher(s)" throughout the book is used only to simplify descriptions and directions. It is not meant to exclude others who work with children. The materials in this book will benefit classroom teachers, but they are equally appropriate for others who work with students to teach social learning.

This book takes a fun, engaging, hands-on approach to social learning. Getting started on games and activities without elaborate verbal or written instructions keeps kids actively learning and developing social cognitive skills. The scope of this teaching includes self-regulation, social communication, and perspective-taking. I recommend beginning with self-regulation, as it is necessary for students to self-regulate in order to attend to learning. Once enough self-regulatory skills have been developed for students to comfortably attend to other learning, social communication and perspective-taking lessons can follow.

This book is organized to include a discussion chapter in each of these three core areas for social emotional learning and an accompanying lesson plan chapter with ten games and activities for each core content area. It is not uncommon for a school year to span about thirty-six weeks. Eliminating the weeks that have alternative scheduling due to holidays and other days off, it is feasible to use these thirty lessons as once-weekly social emotional instruction to span the school year.

An important feature in each lesson plan is What the Research Says, a brief explanation of the research that supports the development of skills in each lesson-specific area. For example, it seems logical that developing perspective-taking skills helps reading comprehension, so a relevant research study accompanies a related lesson plan on perspective-taking. Ready-to-use reproducible templates, charts, and other resources are another helpful feature of this book. Pre-made materials can be a real time-saver when planning and implementing content that is new to teachers and students.

Finally, the content of the lessons contained in this book ranges from critical foundational skills to the integration of more sophisticated, nuanced skills. The lessons are designed for use with a range of ages. Some lessons may include age suggestions, such as with identifying when a "junior" version of a game is available. Most lessons are fun for most ages, even through adulthood, and can be adapted to meet the needs of diverse learners. In some cases, the lessons use familiar games with familiar directions. Rather than focus on *how* to play, this frees up attention for teaching social cognition skills. The lessons are not a "silver bullet." Rather, they are designed for repeated use, allowing for teachers and students to build familiarity and deepen understandings and for students to demonstrate the advancement of their skills over time in a specific activity.

When using this book, be bold, jump in, and teach. Even if it is new, even if mistakes happen, the benefits far outweigh the risks.

Note: *Names and identifying characteristics and details in scenarios that appear in this book have been changed to protect the privacy of individuals.*

Acknowledgments

It is a privilege to be part of a community that values the role of social learning in student success. The Stern Center for Language and Learning provides a nurturing home where knowledge about the whole child combined with clinical expertise in cognitive, linguistic, and academic learning guides teaching practices. I am grateful to this organization, its staff, leadership, board of directors, and generous friends.

My Stern Center colleagues deserve recognition for their stellar support and talents: Blanche Podhajski, president and founder, whose vision inspired this book; Ed Wilkens, who shepherded this project from the beginning; and the entire Social Learning and Communication team, past and present, whose wealth of expertise and creativity have inspired many of the ideas in this book. I'm also grateful to Joan Novelli for her invaluable expertise in guiding this important project to completion, and to Ann Wong for her keen eye and edits.

I am thankful to all of my family and friends, for your patience and support through the years and through the development of this book. I am so very grateful to my siblings for being the kindest, smartest, and most talented human beings on the planet. I love that we are always happier and stronger in any situation when we are together and that we never fight. Few people are so lucky. Even fewer are blessed with a relationship like the one I have with my husband, Joe. Thank you Joe, for sharing all of the humor, friendship, and romance that I thought could never exist in one relationship.

Julie Erdelyi , MA
Director of Social Learning and Communication
Stern Center for Language and Learning

We at the Stern Center take pride in being at the intersection of the heart and science of learning. We have long appreciated the important role social learning plays in that dynamic, and we are pleased to offer this new book as an essential tool to help others recognize and practice such vital pedagogy.

This book is the product of many years and layers of contributions to the Stern Center, its mission, and its services. It is the presentation of Julie Erdelyi's knowledge, expertise, and vision. It is the result of a generous investment from Deborah Schapiro and Lou Polish, an expression of their passionate commitment to enriching the lives of children who struggle navigating their social world. And it was made possible by the creative and cutting-edge environment of the Stern Center itself.

That unique professional environment has been evolving for over thirty-five years, thanks especially to the generous and unflagging support of two families. We extend deep appreciation to the Bernice and Milton Stern Foundation for their foresight and founding donation to the Stern Center in 1983, as well as for their continued loyalty and dedication. Special thanks also to Peter and Margie Stern for tireless support and advocacy on behalf of all learners.

Great thanks also go out to the Hoehl Family Foundation for honoring Cynthia K. Hoehl through the development of the Institute for Excellence bearing her name. Cynthia was a passionate teacher, a dedicated member of the Stern Center's Board of Directors, and a philanthropist who cared deeply about children and educators. The Cynthia K. Hoehl Institute for Excellence serves as a learning hub for parents, educators, and medical personnel. This book is one aspect of the professional learning provided through that institute.

It takes a village, indeed. Wherever and however you define your "village," this book will help you help children better navigate and find more joy there. We are proud to add this book to the professional libraries of educators everywhere, and we are confident that it will inspire meaningful practice.

Blanche Podhajski, PhD
Founder & President, Stern Center for Language and Learning

PUBLISHER'S ACKNOWLEDGMENTS

Corwin gratefully acknowledges the contributions of the following reviewers:

Katie Aeschleman
School Psychologist
Conejo Valley Unified School District
Thousand Oaks, CA

Renee Bernhardt
Education Consultant, Dyslexia Therapist
International Dyslexia Association,
    Georgia Branch
Woodstock, GA

Kimberly Mendenhall Brennan, PhD
Assistant Professor
University of Hawaii, College of Education,
    Department of Special Education
Honolulu, HI

Carrie Carpenter
Reading Specialist/Instructional Coach
Oregon Teacher of the Year, 2003
Redmond, OR

Karen Eastman, PhD
Professor, Special Education
Minnesota State University, Mankato
Mankato, MN

Chris Grace
School Psychologist
St. Mary's County Public Schools
Leonardtown, MD

Katherine Hearn
Classroom Teacher
Colegio Anglo Colombiano
Bogota, Colombia

Dr. Neil MacNeill
Head Master
Ellenbrook Independent Primary School
Ellenbrook, Western Australia

Jacqueline Thousand
Professor Emerita
California State University San Marcos
San Marcos, CA

About the Authors

Julie Erdelyi has a master of arts in special education, with a focus on developmental disabilities, including autism. She has worked at the Stern Center for Language and Learning since 2008 and is currently Director of Social Learning and Communication. Julie also provides social instruction to students with autism and other social cognitive challenges, as well as academic instruction. She has presented workshops and courses on social learning at the BEST Institute (Building Effective Support for Teaching) in Vermont and at the Minnesota State Autism Conference and currently teaches two graduate courses: *Social Cognition 1* and *Supporting Children Through Trauma, Poverty and Adversity*. Julie also regularly offers workshops, including *Managing Anxiety: A Model for Self-Regulation* and *Visual Methods for Improving Perspective-Taking*. She is the author of "Introducing Julie Scrumptious!" (*Autism Asperger's Digest*).

From 1999 through 2008, Julie worked in a specialized classroom for students with autism in Maplewood, Minnesota. The program was new, and the school district supported extensive training from well-known experts, including Jeanette McAfee, Michelle Garcia Winner, Carol Gray, Jed Baker, Temple Grandin, Ami Klin, and Stephen Gutstein. Kari Dunn Buron, and Mitzi Curtis, authors of *The Incredible 5-Point Scale* (AAPC, 2003), were colleagues in Julie's school district and consultants in her classroom.

Currently, Julie consults with schools on implementing evidence-based strategies for social teaching and with parents on how to support their children through social situations at home and in the community. From 2010 through 2018, Julie served on the Vermont Autism Task Force, including four years as cochair, and she is the recipient of the committee's 2018 Appreciation Award. Julie is a member of the Curriculum Advisory Board for Changing Perspectives, a national nonprofit organization that offers cutting-edge resources to schools to educate students about disabilities and create inclusive and empathetic learning environments.

Blanche Podhajski with Deborah Schapiro (left) and Lou Polish (right)

ABOUT THE STERN CENTER FOR LANGUAGE AND LEARNING

The **Stern Center for Language and Learning** is a nonprofit organization dedicated to helping children and adults reach their academic, social, and professional goals. A leader in the field of education and learning, the Stern Center provides comprehensive evaluations and customized instruction for all learners, including those with learning disabilities, language disorders, social learning challenges, autism, attention deficit disorders, communication disorders, giftedness, and learning differences.

Founded in 1983, the Stern Center also provides professional learning for educators. The Stern Center's professional learning programs are offered through the Cynthia K. Hoehl Institute for Excellence (CKHIE), which was established in 2008 to bring research on evidence-based best practices to educators. It is a hub for structured literacy programs through our Orton Gillingham Institute, partnership with Wilson Language Systems, and our Comprehensive Reading Course for Educators online. CKHIE offers grants for professional learning for teachers and intensive instructional services for students. The Stern Center integrates individual and group social learning as well as communication services within its educational programs.

Blanche Podhajski, PhD, founded the Stern Center with a mission to provide direct services for individuals of all ages, to deliver exceptional professional learning programs for educators, and to share research on evidence-based best practices. Dr. Podhajski teaches and consults with educators throughout the country and is a frequent presenter at regional and national conferences. She coauthored the *Comprehensive Reading Course for Educators,* produced by MindPlay, as well as MindPlay's *Teacher Companion*. In addition, she is the coauthor of *Sounds Abound* and *Building Blocks for Literacy*, a course that provides professionals who work with children from birth to age five strategies to promote robust language development and pre-literacy skills.

Why Social Learning? Why Now?

Education is the most powerful weapon which you can use to change the world.

—Nelson Mandela

Nine-year-old boys are super cool. This particular group of three believed they were way too cool to practice the "self-talk" statements their teacher had provided to improve their positive self-talk capabilities. These boys struggled with having reactions that were too big for the size of the problem—for example, tossing a desk when frustrated with a math problem. To help them, their teacher needed to find a way to have them practice self-encouraging statements.

Embracing their competitive nature, she created a card game for them to play called "Chill Out." Like the familiar game "Go Fish," players have to ask other players for certain cards as they try to collect sets: "Do you have any . . ." In this case, the cards are programmed with self-encouraging statements, such as "My parents, my teacher, or my friends will help me if I ask." The very act of playing the game results in each player repeating the self-help statements more than enough times to recall them later. Later the same week, one of the students in this group experienced frustration with a math problem. His desk remained in place.

This real-world example demonstrates the value of providing opportunities for children to learn and practice the skills associated with social learning, such as with resisting impulsive behaviors, sustaining attention on required tasks, managing time, asking for help, and understanding what others feel.

While educators understand the need for social emotional learning, they quickly realize that this type of teaching is very complex. Social emotional learning is not typically addressed in teacher training programs, and when teachers realize the complexity involved, they often avoid this type of instruction because they feel underprepared. *Activities, Games, and Lessons for Social Learning* responds to this need, as well as to what many of today's teachers are finding: That increasing numbers of students are coming to school with much less innate social understanding than in previous years.

Activities, Games, and Lessons for Social Learning is an evidence-based resource that guides educators, specialists, and others who work with children in implementing best practices for social learning. Whether used in the classroom, out-of-school programs, or the home, this collection of hands-on lessons puts social learning theory into practice to help all children develop the social skills that support success in school and beyond.

WHAT IS THE NEED FOR SOCIAL LEARNING?

Social learning challenges are pervasive in today's classrooms. In the last twenty years, teachers have witnessed increases in the population of students with autism spectrum disorder, attention deficit and hyperactivity disorders, emotional disabilities, and social difficulties in the absence of diagnosis. Why?

Much of the answer to that question remains unknown, although research continues into the possible causes, including the following:

- The impact of increasing use of screen technology (Lissak, 2018)

- A rise in the prevalence of autism (Baio et al., 2018)

- Steeply rising opiate addiction rates (Ghertner & Groves, 2018)

- The significant impact of poverty, hunger, and homelessness on the well-being of children (Johnson, Riis, & Noble, 2016)

In the past, social cognitive challenges were commonly thought of as being limited to people with autism spectrum disorder or intellectual disabilities. That is no longer the case, and taking a closer look at influences on social cognitive development opens up several possible reasons. For example, technology is advancing at a rate faster than we can study the impact on children. Information is emerging, however, about the influence of screen time on children's physical and psychological health. The immediate gratification that technology can offer may negatively impact the development of skills for waiting, empathizing, and recognizing other points of view. In addition to a rising prevalence of autism, undiagnosed autism in early years can result in years of missed information that is critical to social development. In babies and young children with autism, the brain is not attending to critical elements of social communication, such as facial expressions, reciprocity, and emotions. Similarly, the experience of early childhood trauma may cause the child's brain to be hypervigilant about details that are not relevant to typical social brain development. Neglect can also have a powerful negative impact on an infant's developing brain, reducing the child's ability to engage in dynamic reciprocal communication exchanges.

SOCIAL LEARNING AND ACADEMIC SUCCESS

Research supports the link between social learning skills and academic success. The Aspen Institute's National Commission on Social, Emotional, and Academic Development recently brought together a 28-member council to "develop a consensus view on what research says about integrating social, emotional, and academic development" (Jones & Kahn, 2017). The Consensus Statements of Evidence that came out of this initiative, summarized in *The Evidence Base for How We Learn: Supporting Students' Social, Emotional, and Academic Development* (2017), provide an evidence-based case that establishes the importance of integrating social and emotional learning in preK–12 academic instruction to improve outcomes for every student. As previously mentioned, Durlak et al. (2011) showed that achievement test scores for participants in social emotional learning programs were 11 percent higher than for other students.

The material in this book supports teachers in helping their students achieve standards-based learning goals. While specific educational standards may vary from state to state, many of the expectations for children's learning share a similar focus. The chart below identifies examples of some of these common expectations and standards for student learning as they relate to the content areas in this book.

Self-Regulation	Social Communication	Perspective-Taking
• Constructively express feelings, preferences, and needs	• Ask questions about what a speaker says	• Recognize and evaluate author's or speaker's point of view
• Persevere in solving problems	• Use language expressively and persuasively	• Classify and categorize
• Analyze how characters respond to events in a story	• Narrate events in the order in which they occurred	• Determine main ideas in text and identify how they are supported by details
	• Participate in collaborative conversations	

Educators are seeking evidence-based methods that help them help their students. Current research on social cognitive development is woven throughout this book, including relevant supports for each of thirty practical lessons on self-regulation, social communication, and perspective-taking. This research provides a foundation for understanding the development of core social cognitive processes.

WHAT IS THE IDEAL APPROACH TO SOCIAL LEARNING?

The best recipe for helping children to effectively improve social development involves a combination of a knowledgeable instructor (educators, parents, guidance counselors, therapists, extended family—all are welcome!) paired with engaging, ideally fun activities as a platform for the learning to take place. Patricia Wolfe, leading authority on translating neuroscience research to practical application in education, and others have provided excellent strategies for multimodal, engaged learning practices over the years. This book places a priority on learning through play as a means of targeting the three major areas of social learning: self-regulation, social communication, and perspective-taking. A brief introduction to each follows.

SELF-REGULATION

Self-regulation is a person's ability to obtain and maintain the optimal balance between alertness and relaxation that is needed in a given situation. The cognitive skills required to do this requires forethought, problem-solving, and self-reflection. The physical requirements include sensory awareness, regulation, and practice.

SOCIAL COMMUNICATION

Social communication involves all of the aspects of our communication with one another. It includes the words we use and much more. Critical components of communication include both expressive and receptive use of body language, facial expressions, voice tone, prosody, and pragmatics. While an interaction between teacher and student may not necessarily be viewed as "social" but instead as academic, for the purposes of this book, social communication is best categorized as all types and styles of communication between people in any situation.

PERSPECTIVE-TAKING

Perspective-taking is the ability for a person to understand the thoughts and feelings of other people. In autism, there is a known challenge in the development of theory of mind, identified by Simon Baron-Cohen (2000) as "being able to infer mental states (beliefs, desires, intentions, imagination, emotions, etc.) that cause action" (p. 3). Other conditions, too, can impact the natural development of theory of mind, and when this happens, direct instruction becomes critically important.

For each of these key areas, readers will find a thorough discussion of the topic in the chapters that follow, along with a corresponding set of ready-to-use lesson plans that support explicit instruction and "learning by doing." This approach is grounded in research, summarized in "Enhancing and Practicing Executive Function Skills With Children From Infancy to Adolescence" (2014). It is also informed by this author's hands-on experience of over 28 years with students, from the toddler age through young adults.

ABOUT THE LESSONS IN THIS BOOK

The lessons in this book include directions and the optimal number of participants for the purposes of teaching social learning skills. Many of the games and activities in these lessons can be adapted for a full-class approach, though increasing the number of players/participants may also increase wait time and reduce engagement. For example, the game Suspend (see pp. 24–26) can be adapted for a large group by having one person at a time roll the die, place a rod, and return to the group while the next person takes a turn.

WHAT DOES SOCIAL LEARNING LOOK LIKE FOR STUDENTS?

For students, we can simplify the key areas of social learning into three steps: Listen, care, change. When students are with other people (every situation is social), they must *listen* for social information and feedback, *care* about the information they receive, and then willingly *change* their words and actions if necessary to maintain positive social interactions. Students might think of these steps like a video game, advancing from level one to more challenging levels to get where they want to go. A more advanced version of this three-step skillset is predict, care, change. Here, students *predict* what others around them might think and feel, they *care* about those thoughts and feelings, and they *change* their words and actions accordingly if needed.

"Listen" and "predict" in these examples are perspective-taking skills. "Caring" refers to self-regulation, and "change" refers to a combination of self-regulation and social communication. The chapters in this book elaborate on the definitions of each of these three core areas of social cognition and provide practical instructions for games and activities that will help students develop their social cognitive skills.

The activities in this resource can be used in any order. However, for students who struggle with self-regulation, it may be best to begin with the corresponding chapters. Chapter 1, which follows, provides a thorough background on self-regulation. Lesson plans for teaching self-regulation (Chapter 2) begin on page 23.

Teaching Self-Regulation

CHAPTER ONE

Self-Regulation
The Basics

If you are distressed by anything external, the pain is not due to the thing itself, but to your estimate of it; and this you have the power to revoke at any moment.

—Marcus Aurelius, *Meditations*

Gabi:	(Gathers several of the game pieces into her hands and quietly disengages from playing.)
Micky:	Oh, look at this! I can go! (Moves game piece three spaces.)
Zoli:	My turn.
Gabi:	(Gathers the neckline of her shirt and sinks her head down inside it.)
Zoli:	Hey, Micky, I don't think she likes this.
Micky:	Gabi, what's wrong?
Gabi:	(Laughing from inside her shirt.) You guys are just making me laugh too much!
Micky:	If you're laughing, you must be happy, so why are you hiding in your shirt?
Zoli:	I think she's laughing at you!
Micky:	Maybe I said something really funny.

(Continued)

> (Continued)
>
> **Gabi:** (Growls from inside her shirt.) Now I'm getting really angry!
>
> **Zoli:** (Pats Gabi on the shoulder.) It's okay, Gabi.
>
> **Gabi:** (Roars at Zoli from inside her shirt.)
>
> **Micky:** Let's put these pieces away and find something else to play.

When Gabi began to disengage from the game, she was beginning to escalate. Hiding inside her shirt, she began quietly escaping the stressful situation. Her friends, meaning well, tried to discover what was bothering her, but the combination of added attention and talking only increased her stress. Typical of many types of escalation, her emotions were not well regulated, and she started with laughter and ended with a roar. She also showed how challenging it can be to communicate with calm words when feeling upset. As Gabi grows and learns to self-regulate, she will gain more control of her communication and emotional responses during stressful events. This chapter provides an in-depth understanding of self-regulation and offers strategies for directly teaching self-regulation skills to students.

WHAT IS SELF-REGULATION?

There are many definitions of self-regulation. According to Nigg (2017), self-regulation is "the intrinsic processes aimed at adjusting mental and physiological state adaptively to context." Or stated simply, self-regulation is our ability to maintain the balance of alertness and calmness needed for a given situation. This involves the brain and the sensory system working together to employ the cognitive and physical strategies needed to understand what this balance should look like and then do what is necessary to either increase the level of alertness or calmness.

On the playground, for example, students can use heightened alertness to move their bodies rapidly and run around and play while maintaining enough calmness to avoid crashing into each other. In the classroom, students need to maintain enough alertness to attend to academic material or the teacher's directions while using enough calmness to fit the expectations for the environment, such as remaining seated at a desk or using a quiet voice.

The cognitive components of self-regulation include executive function skills and coping skills (such as "self-talk") needed to successfully coach oneself through completing a task.

UNDERSTANDING SELF-REGULATION: STRESS AND THE BRAIN

An understanding of self-regulation begins with taking a look at how the brain functions under stress. The amygdala acts as a sort of triage nurse as information comes into the brain. It sorts out the information by levels of threat. If incoming information is perceived as threatening, the lower part of the brain, the cerebellum becomes more active. This part of the brain is responsible for autonomic functions such as breathing, heart rate, and our survival instincts: fight, flight, or freeze.

When we consider the evolutionary function of a well-developed fight, flight, or freeze response, it seems like a positive aspect of human development. However, when we are around others who are experiencing it, our experience is not only unpleasant, it can be dangerous. Fight responses include punching, hitting, kicking, biting, swearing, and verbal attacks. Flight responses include bolting from the classroom or building and running away or hiding inside clothing or separate spaces. Freeze responses can include refusal or inability to speak as well as ignoring others.

When teachers think about students who are punching, swearing, bolting, and ignoring, they often become concerned about the behaviors and may wonder if the behaviors are deliberate. By definition, "deliberate" means that the student has thought about and planned the behavior. Due to the brain function involved with a fight, flight, or freeze response, this is an impossibility! Granted, people do exhibit deliberate behaviors—and self-regulation can be used to manage those as well. However, it is the unplanned, uncontrolled response that self-regulation is so helpful at preventing.

While the increased activity in the cerebellum is necessary for survival, there are activities that the cerebellum does not control. That part of the brain does not make decisions or solve problems. The frontal lobe of the brain is responsible for the higher level of thought required for problem-solving. The problem is, if the cerebellum is activated due to perceived or real threat, how does a person shift brain activity to make the frontal lobe more active? The answer involves considering how the stressful information was received in the brain in the first place . . . the sensory system!

UNDERSTANDING SELF-REGULATION: ATTENTIONAL CHALLENGES

When students are experiencing difficulty with concentration and an inability to be still, even for brief periods of time, parents and teachers may suspect or seek a diagnosis of attention deficit/hyperactivity disorder (AD/HD). In cases where this condition is present, the student feels an internal sense of exhaustion. Constant attention shifting and movement are the child's efforts to stay alert. Therefore, healthcare providers may prescribe a stimulant medication, such as Ritalin, which increases that internal sense of alertness, diminishing the need for the child to move and constantly shift attention. This treatment is effective for many; however, what happens when symptoms mimic AD/HD, but the cause is actually a heightened stress response?

When a child experiences frequent stress sufficient enough to activate the hypothalamic-pituitary-adrenal (HPA) axis with regularity, that system begins to adapt to frequent activation and can become overactive when any perceived stressor occurs. A loud voice in a classroom, the sound of a door closing, or a stern tone are all stressors that many can manage without needing to fight, flee, or freeze. But when the stress response system is overactive, it activates for experiences that others tolerate without a stress response.

If some students are experiencing a heightened stress response due to trauma history and the response itself causes problems with concentration and elevated heart rate, then a stimulant is likely to make matters worse. Therefore, it is extremely important for teachers and parents who are observing students struggling with regulation to consider all possible origins of the problem. A thorough health assessment, including developmental history conducted by a pediatric health care provider knowledgeable about trauma and AD/HD is the best initial approach when teachers and parents are concerned about attention challenges.

UNDERSTANDING SELF-REGULATION: TRAUMA AND STRESS RESPONSE

In her TEDMED talk, "How Childhood Trauma Affects Health Across a Lifetime" (2014), pediatrician Nadine Burke Harris, MD, discusses the health impacts of childhood trauma, or adverse childhood experiences (ACEs), and toxic stress. Burke Harris describes the central stress response as the "hypothalamic-pituitary-adrenal axis," medical terminology used to identify the pathway of the "fight or flight" stress response system. The hypothalamus sends a signal to the pituitary gland, which signals the release of adrenaline. Adrenaline increases heart and breathing rates, allowing for the faster exchange of oxygen between muscles and the circulatory system, which allows for the person experiencing this response to fight or flee quickly and effectively.

In 1998, the *American Journal of Preventive Medicine* published the study "Relationship of Childhood Abuse and Household Dysfunction to Many of the Leading Causes of Death in Adults. The Adverse Childhood Experiences (ACE) Study." Twenty years later, parents, teachers, and healthcare providers are still learning about this seminal study and the health impacts of ACEs.

Burke Harris likens childhood trauma to lead exposure. The greater the exposure, the greater the health risk. Once exposure is discovered, abatement of adversity, as with lead, is necessary for improved health outcomes. More important than the specific types of adversity, teachers, parents, and healthcare professionals need to focus on how much adversity a child has experienced.

Examples of adverse childhood experiences include the following:

- Physical abuse

- Sexual abuse

- Emotional abuse

- Physical neglect

- Emotional neglect

- Exposure to domestic violence

- Household substance abuse

- Household mental illness

- Parental separation or divorce

- Incarcerated household member

In recent years, school systems have worked to become "trauma informed." Teachers and parents increasingly recognize the impact of childhood trauma in today's classrooms and are working to learn more and to provide safe, effective interventions to improve student learning and outcomes. Teaching self-regulation seems, on the surface, a relatively simple task: Demonstrate ways for kids to calm down when they are stressed, and they will automatically repeat these skills as needed. However, below the surface, the process is quite complex.

Effective methods for teaching include using a combination of cognitive and sensory-based strategies and increasing understanding of the origins of dysregulation. Physical therapists, occupational therapists, behavior analysts, mental health counselors, health care providers, educators, and parents can all have valuable input as to appropriate interventions for meeting each child's unique, individual needs.

LEARN MORE ABOUT ACEs

Additional resources on adverse childhood experiences (ACEs) and the hypothalamic-pituitary-adrenal axis include the following:

- *The Deepest Well: Healing the Long-Term Effects of Childhood Adversity*, by Dr. Nadine Burke Harris (Houghton Mifflin Harcourt, 2018)

- "How Childhood Trauma Affects Health Across a Lifetime," Nadine Burke Harris, MD, TEDMED, 2014

- https://www.ted.com/talks/nadine_burke_harris_how_childhood_trauma_affects_health_across_a_lifetime?language=en

- *Resilience: The Biology of Stress and the Science of Hope*, documentary by KPJR Films

Basically, a teacher can consider self-regulation as requiring skill development in two areas: (1) cognitive skills (such as coping skills and executive functions) and (2) sensory regulation strategies developed with knowledge of the sensory system; fight, flight, or freeze; stress responses in the brain and the impacts of adversity and trauma on development. The development of self-regulation skills prevents undesirable behaviors, so a discussion about self-regulation frequently includes discussion of behavior, as well as factors related to behavior. Understanding behavior starts with understanding that behaviors serve a function and understanding that positive behavior supports can increase positive behaviors. This chapter presents explicit, detailed information about each of these areas, beginning with behaviors.

FUNCTIONS OF BEHAVIORS AND INTERVENTIONS

All behaviors serve a function. In other words, every action has a desired outcome, whether the student is cognitively aware of the outcome or not. For the sorts of behaviors teachers see on a daily basis, which may be annoying but not particularly harmful (blurting out answers, excessive movement, grabbing others' belongings), positive behavioral interventions and supports (PBIS) can be the most effective approach.

FINDING THE FUNCTION OF A BEHAVIOR: THE MOTIVATION ASSESSMENT SCALE

Durand and Crimmins (1992) developed an easy to use, readily available manual and questionnaire called the Motivation Assessment Scale, which teachers, parents, and staff can use to make a quick, objective hypothesis about the function of a problematic behavior. The key to using this form successfully is to identify a highly specific behavior and then have three or more individuals (teachers, parents, and staff, who have all observed the target behavior) complete the form for the same behavior. "Crashing body into other students, walls, and tables while standing in the lunch line" is highly specific, whereas "crashing into people and things" is much less specific. This tool produces the best results when the identified behavior is highly specific.

Durand and Crimmins (1992) identified the following four categories to describe the functions of all behaviors: sensory, escape, attention, tangible (SEAT). The basic theory behind dealing with problematic or maladaptive behaviors is to discover which function is being served when the child carries out the behavior.

- **Sensory:** A child who expresses pain or runs from the room when hearing a sudden, loud noise may be exhibiting an auditory sensitivity. Sensory needs are best addressed under the guidance of occupational or physical therapists. (For more information, see The Sensory System, p. 20.)

- **Escape:** A child who crumples up a math worksheet and throws it across the room may be seeking an escape from math. Escape can be a challenging function to address, but if the teacher can guide the child to choose only a couple of problems on the worksheet to complete and then take a break (escape), the child learns that escape can be gained in a more adaptive way. The tricky part is to find the balance of building in an "escape plan" that children can use before they feel the need to create their own.

- **Attention:** Children who constantly follow the teacher around or engage in nonstop bids for conversation may be seeking attention. If they learn that they can receive positive attention for waiting or remaining quiet, they will likely change the behavior to get this need met.

- **Tangible:** The child who is climbing on top of the refrigerator at home to gain access to the cookie jar is seeking a tangible. Climbing on top of the refrigerator is dangerous, so the child needs to be given strategies or taught other methods of gaining the cookie.

The following analogy represents what teachers experience when trying to guess the function of a behavior. Imagine taking a newspaper and holding it up against the end of your nose: The text is impossible to read. Similarly, it may be possible to make out a headline or two on a newspaper sitting on a table across the room, but the text of the article is still impossible to read. Along these lines, guessing the function of a specific behavior is generally a bad idea and frequently unsuccessful.

The teacher may know a student very well and be extremely close to the situation, making it impossible to maintain the objectivity required to accurately determine the function of a behavior. The same teacher may also be aware of a behavior that is occurring in a classroom of thirty kids and not be close enough to the situation to determine the function. Therefore, it is important for teachers to use an objective means of determining the function of a problematic behavior such as the Motivation Assessment Scale (described previously in this section), consultation with a specialist, or a Functional Behavior Assessment.

FINDING THE FUNCTION OF A BEHAVIOR: FUNCTIONAL BEHAVIOR ASSESSMENT

A Functional Behavior Assessment (FBA) is an objective assessment that is conducted by educational teams that may include the school psychologist, classroom teacher, special educator, speech and occupational therapists, parents, behavior analysts, and others. FBAs require extensive information gathering, observations, and trial interventions, leading the team to develop a hypothesis for the function of the behavior, which is then systematically tested, with results observed and analyzed. The team uses the information to develop an effective behavior support plan. Sometimes, conducting a full FBA may feel time- and cost-prohibitive. While there are instances in which a full FBA may be required by law (von Ravensberg & Blakely, 2014), there may be times when a team is seeking information about the function of a behavior and is choosing not to conduct a full FBA. At such times, the team may use other objective means of proactively determining the function of a behavior, such as the Motivation Assessment Scale.

A FRAMEWORK FOR BEHAVIORAL INTERVENTIONS

Established in 1997, PBIS is an evidence-based framework for educators to help students improve behavior (Horner, Sugai, & Anderson, 2010). PBIS emphasizes teaching expectations for positive behavior over punishing undesirable behaviors. Often used classroom-wide and schoolwide, PBIS strategies are also effective for use with individuals. PBIS strategies align with principles of applied behavior analysis (ABA)—increase the desired behaviors, and the undesired behaviors will automatically decrease (Hieneman, 2015). In order to increase a desired behavior, the teacher needs to use rewards that are motivating to the particular students. Following is an example of a classroom-wide positive behavior intervention.

> *Whenever the teacher sees a student performing a desired behavior (such as sitting quietly, working diligently, handing in an assignment, helping a classmate), the student is invited to place a "Terrific Ticket" in a box. A Terrific Ticket is simply a small piece of paper that children write their names on before placing it in the box. With regularity (weekly, for example), the teacher draws names from the box and rewards those students with the option to select an activity or to have free time.*

Classroom management of this strategy is simple, requiring little planning or effort, but the result is highly motivating for students. This is an easy system for a teacher to prepare and manage, requiring only a few small notepads and a box (kept in a designated location in the room) that can be emptied with whatever regularity (monthly, for example) that the teacher prefers. The more times a child's name goes into the box, the higher the likelihood of being selected. Students constantly strive to engage in behaviors that will result in more tickets in the box.

In a schoolwide model of this strategy, teachers might place a marble in a jar while announcing the desired behavior just observed. The marbles are counted regularly (perhaps monthly), and when the school reaches a target number, the entire school earns a fun activity, such as a pizza party or pajama day.

The use of proactive strategies as part of the implementation of positive behavioral interventions and supports are the most effective way to prevent undesired behavior, as students will automatically have to decrease undesired behaviors to increase the desired ones. When more explicit problematic behaviors continue to recur, teachers may need to look more closely at the function of those behaviors to support students in substituting a more adaptive, tolerable way of meeting their needs.

COGNITIVE SKILLS

Cognitive skills for self-regulation can be divided into two areas: coping skills and executive function skills. In essence, these are the thinking strategies students need to either motivate themselves to take action or to calm themselves so they can maintain the necessary communication and actions for the situation. Through guided instruction and practice, students can develop cognitive skills for coping and executive functions to help them self-regulate in situations that cause increased stress, confusion, self-doubt, or emotional dysregulation. It's critically important for students to proactively practice using these skills outside of the stressful situation, such as while playing a game, to help them build these new and useful habits.

COGNITIVE SKILLS: COPING SKILLS

Coping skills can be used by anyone at any time. They require no special equipment or accommodations. Therefore, they can be used as an emergency response to acute stress, or they can be used as part of a daily practice for self-regulation. To ensure that these strategies are accessible to students at any time, the list of strategies must be limited to those that have been proven to work over time and those that do not require specialized space, in-the-moment interactions, or equipment. Examples include the following:

- Breathing exercises
- Meditation/mindfulness
- Taking space
- Self-talk
- Expressing thoughts verbally to available listener or written on paper

Each coping skill should be explicitly taught at a time *other than when the skill is needed*. Many people presume others' competence with breathing, meditation, or self-talk. However, the efficacy of these skills increases when time has been devoted to learning how to do them. One type of breathing technique includes breathing in, holding briefly, then breathing out more slowly than the in-breath. It is important to practice different styles of breathing with students so they can apply the coping skill automatically when under stress.

COGNITIVE SKILLS: EXECUTIVE FUNCTIONS

In "Enhancing and Practicing Executive Function Skills From Infancy to Adolescence," the Harvard Center for the Developing Child (2014) defines executive function and self-regulation as "the mental processes that enable us to plan, focus attention, remember instructions, and juggle multiple tasks successfully." The article compares the brain to an air traffic control system: "Just as an air traffic control system at a busy airport manages the arrivals and departures of many aircraft on multiple runways, the brain needs this skill set to filter distractions, prioritize tasks, set and achieve goals, and control impulses." As with many cognitive capabilities, the executive functions are not present at birth but are developed with time and practice. Understanding the intricacies of executive functions can help teachers design and use activities that supply students with the experiences and practice necessary for their brains to develop these skills.

In *Social Foundations of Thought and Action: A Social Cognitive Theory*, Albert Bandura (1986) identified forethought and self-reflective capabilities as necessary aspects of executive functions in social cognitive development.

Forethought Capability

Forethought capability is a student's ability to plan ahead. This can be as simple as planning to walk around an obstacle in one's path or as complicated as collecting the right book, pencil, paper, folder, worksheet, or other combination of materials needed to start working on an academic assignment. It also applies to everyday life. Turning on the oven to let it preheat for baking prior to collecting and mixing ingredients, organizing a shopping list by categories to make walking through the grocery store more efficient, and turning off the electricity before changing a light switch are all examples of the need for solidly developed forethought capabilities.

Forethought capability requires internal verbal mediation. A person must be able to think through and label what is going to be needed to complete a task. When people experience stress, language capabilities diminish, thereby reducing forethought capability. Having students practice forethought can help them develop increased automaticity in these skills so that when stress arises, the practice is more automatic and requires less verbal mediation.

Consider the act of driving: When people drive, they complete many series of steps to carry out seemingly simple tasks, such as making a turn:

- Step on the brake to slow the vehicle.

- Activate the turn signal to show the intended action to other drivers.

- Look in all directions for possible obstacles or dangers.

- Wait if necessary for other drivers.

- Turn the wheel to the desired angle.

- Gently increase speed to complete the turn.

- Return the steering wheel to straighten out the car.

Learning to drive requires practice, and in the beginning, an instructor verbally mediates each step before it occurs so that the driver learns the sequence. With a little practice, these steps become more automatic. Drivers can think through the steps using self-talk, and with more practice, they often report driving skills as "automatic" or happening without thinking about it.

See SKIP-BO lesson plan (pp. 45–46) to learn more about using this card game to teach self-regulatory skills.

The same is true for learning to read, write, calculate math problems, get dressed, or tie one's shoes. SKIP-BO is an example of a game that provides practice with several levels of forethought practice and impulse control. Playing this card game with students can help increase self-regulatory skills, including forethought and planning, problem-solving, inhibitory control, and self-reflection.

Self-Reflective Capability

Self-reflective capability is the ability to reflect on words or actions recently carried out and ask, "How did that work out for me?" It is an individual's capacity to evaluate the effectiveness of a problem-solving approach in achieving a desired outcome. Therefore, the person must first recognize and label the desired goal, consider the action used to achieve the goal, decide whether or not the goal was achieved, and decide whether the goal could be achieved more efficiently or easily.

In the game Uno, for example, players must choose to play a card that matches the pile by either color or number. They make a choice, and the next player may benefit from that choice or even win the game based on the card played. While there is luck involved as well as attention to others' cards, the process of recognizing how one's actions achieved an outcome is helpful in shaping future decision-making. Teachers and parents can help to prompt this self-reflection during game play. "Look at the card you decided to play. Now I cannot play my card! That means you are closer to winning. Do you think you made a good decision? Yes, you did!"

See Uno lesson plan (pp. 41–42) to learn more about using this card game to teach self-regulatory skills.

Similarly, when a student recognizes an error of any kind and says, "Oh no! I meant to . . . ," this is an opportunity for a teacher or parent to respond, "You are using self-reflection, and that is a skill that will help you to avoid mistakes or make better decisions next time."

Impulse Control

Impulse control is required when, despite solid forethought capabilities, internal and external distractions occur along the way. For example, cell phones are a common distraction for older students. Direct instruction and practice for managing distractions is necessary. Having students recognize and list things that commonly distract them and then develop strategies for managing these distractions as an explicit lesson outside of the situations in which these distractions occur can raise student awareness of the distractors as they occur in life. This can help students more readily access the strategies they need to maintain focus on a goal. Going back to the cell phone distraction, for example, students have to (1) recognize the cell phone as a distraction and (2) use a replacement thought each time they feel an impulse to look at the phone, such as "I can wait to look at my phone. If there's an emergency, a teacher will tell me about it."

To promote impulse control, such as with rushing to line up for lunch, engage students briefly in energetic movement (while being safe)—tapping their hands and feet or even running in place. Then announce, "Change your thinking!" as a prompt for students to change from showing what their bodies look like when they have too much energy, to showing what they look like when they are regulated (such as standing or sitting quietly). Praise the shift in thinking and movement, encouraging students to feel empowered that they can control impulses.

The Reaction Energy Cycles visuals provided in this book are a valuable tool for teaching impulse control. They can be used to help kids understand the comparison between what their bodies feel like when they slow down an angry reaction versus what they feel like when they have a fast, impulsive, angry reaction. Full-sized versions of these visuals are available on pp. 125–126.

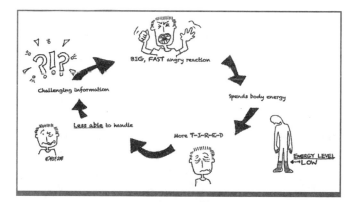

Figure 1.1   Reaction Energy Cycles Visual 1

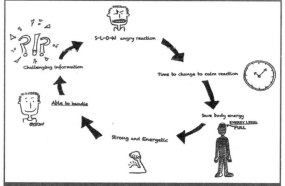

Figure 1.2   Reaction Energy Cycles Visual 2

Figure 1.1 and Figure 1.2 created by Kathleen Fechter. Used with permission.

Several classic childhood games are helpful for improving impulse control as well. Mother May I?, Simon Says, and Red Light, Green Light all require players to attend to a stimulus and follow it, regardless of the internal impulse to carry out an action. Players need to attend to the impulse and then modify their actions based on the stimulus provided. Once students have had multiple opportunities to practice impulse control in fun ways, teachers and parents can identify and label when this skill is needed in other areas. Students can then apply the well-practiced and easily recognized skill to the new task. The following example is a familiar one in classrooms:

> When the teacher announces, "time to line up for lunch," several students get up and rush to be the first in line, without considering their belongings, the designated line leader, or other predetermined organization of this event. The impulse to "be first" is often so strong that kids cannot resist it. If students have previously practiced a game

such as Mother May I?, the teacher can announce, "Using your best Mother May I? skills, let's line up for lunch." Following the cue, students respond by asking, "Mother, may I ____ [put away books, stand up, push in my chair, etc.]?" The teacher can respond by giving students "permission" to carry out each step of the process in order, redirecting students as needed by replying, "No, but you may ___."

For older students, simply include impulse control in the prompt. For example, say, "I am going to ask you to exchange your paper with another student, and while you do so, I would like you to suppress the impulse to talk." A few students will typically say a couple of words, but they have a much easier time resisting the urge when given the reminder before the direction.

THE SENSORY SYSTEM

Are we rewarding undesirable behaviors whenever we teach self-regulation strategies? This is a common question. Most teachers want to avoid the practice of giving students "breaks" for misbehaving. This is a wise approach and supports the need to have the sensory aspects of self-regulation guided by an occupational or physical therapist. If we think about sensory input that is perceived as threatening as the cause of a "fight, flight, or freeze" protective response, it is logical to think about sensory input that is pleasurable as causing a release of dopamine and increasing frontal lobe activity in the brain.

The challenge occurs when we see students exhibiting protective responses and we need them to seek pleasurable sensory input to shift the brain activity. In the case of physical or verbal aggression, such as one student hitting another, or in the case of self-harm, it may be necessary to teach students the difference between "in the moment" (anywhere, at any time) emergency coping strategies and sensory regulation strategies that they can use proactively to balance the needs of the sensory system.

There continues to be controversy over the evidence base behind sensory integration and the role of school professionals in teaching it. So without addressing sensory integration programs or teaching, it is important to recognize that the sensory system is responsible for getting information into the brain. Information comes into the brain through eight senses: taste, touch, smell, hearing, vision, proprioception, vestibular sensation, and interoception. Most people are familiar with the first five senses, so the remaining three—proprioception, vestibular sensation, and interoception—deserve some attention:

- **Proprioception:** Proprioception is the sensation of pressure in the joints. It can be achieved by squeezing, chewing, carrying heavy objects, doing push-ups, and many other activities. Proprioception has the effect on the sensory system of alerting it or calming it—whichever is needed in the moment.

- **Vestibular Sensation:** Vestibular sensation is the sensation of movement, such as with walking, running, spinning, and rocking. Vestibular input to the sensory system has the effect of alerting the sensory system. Even without knowing about vestibular input, teachers are quite intuitive about using movement to help students stay alert.

- **Interoception:** Interoception is the sensory input from sensations that arise from inside the body, such as hunger, headache, or even the need to urinate.

When the sensory system is functioning well, the sensations people experience can be well-tolerated. Sometimes a part or parts of the sensory system can under-receive or over-receive information. So many people experience irritation at the sensation of a tag inside a shirt against their skin, for example, that many clothing companies now print the information that used to be on a tag directly on the fabric inside the shirt.

At times, the sensory experience may interfere with a student's ability to function well in a classroom. A student who experiences tactile defensiveness, such as described with the clothing tag, may also seek out touching people and may push or crash into people or things. A student who experiences auditory defensiveness may try to drown out the sound of others who are talking by making repetitive noises. Ironically, these behaviors are disruptive to the classroom environment, although the student is desperately trying to self-regulate.

When problematic behaviors are the result of sensory input, an occupational or physical therapist can design a "sensory diet," a sequence of activities that provides balancing input into the sensory system, thereby reducing the student's need to use problematic behaviors to self-regulate. Simple accommodations, such as the availability of noise canceling headphones, can eliminate irritating auditory input and reduce the resulting extraneous noise-making.

SENSORY REGULATION STRATEGIES

Sensory regulation strategies should be used proactively to help balance the sensory system when a specific sensory difference has been identified. Standardized assessments, such as the Sensory Profile (Dunn, 1999), and consultation with trained professionals, such as physical and occupational therapists, are helpful tools to identify specific sensory differences. The goal, when a sensory difference is identified, is to create a sensory diet that will fulfill the sensory needs in an adaptive and functional way.

For example, individuals with auditory sensitivity may have such an adverse reaction to certain sounds (such as buzzing lights or whirring ventilation) that they create their own "white noise" by constantly humming to block out those sounds. This can be annoying to others. Proactively using hearing protection when the offensive auditory input is likely to occur can prevent the humming from occurring in the first place and protect the individual from the painful auditory stimuli. Similarly, students who constantly mouth items may be alerting their sensory system as a result of feeling internally tired. Alerting the system through planned, regularly scheduled movement or pressure-inducing activities can thereby reduce students' need to alert themselves through gustatory input.

Sensory regulation strategies can certainly be used in response to aversive stimuli. However, a proactive approach with known sensory differences will be most effective in reducing problematic behaviors. This also avoids the impression that the desirable sensory input is immediately available when those behaviors increase.

The following suggestions, based on recommendations that have worked for my many students over the last 20 years, are intended for informational purposes only. They are not intended to be prescriptive. Professional treatment and consultation from a physical or occupational therapist is recommended for individual needs.

Table 1.1   Sensory Regulation Strategies

Sensory Area	Suggested Strategies
Auditory (hearing)	• Music or white noise on headphones: classical, new age, nature sounds (instrumental/no lyrics) • Noise canceling headphones
Gustatory (taste)	• Foods that are "alerting" (for example, sour, minty, crunchy, or chewy foods)
Olfactory (smell)	• Aromatherapy, such as through a diffuser or stuffed animal • Smells or odors that have associations with pleasure or calmness
Visual (sight)	• Dim lighting • Reduced clutter; reduced visual stimulation • Sunglasses for bright lighting • Self-guided movement of head or body to add visual stimuli
Tactile (touch)	• Reduce or eliminate tactile stimuli, such as clothing tags and seams • Use firm touch, which can be less aversive than light touch • Ask to touch; make sure person is prepared for touch; avoid sudden surprise by touching
Interoception (sensations arising internally, such as hunger or headache)	• Explicit teaching and regular check-ins to raise awareness of sensations
Vestibular (sensation of movement)	• Swinging, spinning, rocking, walking, running, jumping
Proprioception (sensation of pressure in the joints)	• Hand squeezes, push-ups, most yoga positions, hugs/handholding • Weighted vests, ankle weights, weighted blanket

The chapter that follows, "Lesson Plans for Teaching Self-Regulation," offers ten lesson plans for activities and games to teach self-regulation skills, providing for the "in the moment" learning and practice children need to generalize skills in new situations. As you use these activities and games with students, keep the following tips in mind:

• Start with the positives! When kids are struggling with self-regulation, they can be very sensitive and self-critical. Keeping an upbeat, positive, "we can do this" attitude throughout the teaching and learning keeps kids engaged and motivated.

• The games and activities can be presented in any order. Feel free to use the ones that might be most appealing to the learner first.

• Stick with it. Self-regulation is learned with repetition and practice. While significant progress may happen quickly, time is necessary for sustained progress.

• Refer to What Does the Research Say? in each lesson to learn more about how the games and activities support the development of self-regulation skills, such as positive self-talk, self-control, and attention shifting.

CHAPTER TWO

Lesson Plans for Teaching Self-Regulation

Table 2.1   Self-Regulation Lesson Plans Overview

Game/Activity	Areas of Focus	Page
Suspend	Feel suspense increase and decrease	24
Taboo	Inhibitory control	27
Tenzi	Fast, frenzied movement versus slow, controlled movement	29
Chill Out	Positive self-talk	33
Flexibility Points	Increase flexibility, decrease rigid thinking	36
Balloon Release	Letting go of difficult thoughts	38
Uno	Changes can happen quickly	41
Personal Space Role-Play	Learn about personal space	43
SKIP-BO	Executive functions, planning, inhibitory control	45
Spit	Coordinating fast movement and thinking about others	47

Lesson I: Suspend

SUSPEND

With repeated play, this classic balancing game helps students build awareness about the physical feelings associated with increased stress. Teaching students to notice these physical symptoms can help them more quickly recognize when their stress levels are increasing.

OBJECTIVES

Students will increase their awareness of feelings of rising suspense (stress, anxiety) while controlling their speed of movement and breathing.

WHAT DOES THE RESEARCH SAY?

In a game of Suspend, placing each rod on the structure requires slow, balanced movements, also known as "effortful control." Effortful control Is when we inhibit our initial instinctive response, and instead, use a less dominant but more thoughtful and controlled response. Eisenberg et al. (2007) conducted a longitudinal study that showed effortful control to be a powerful predictor of children's social-emotional functioning.

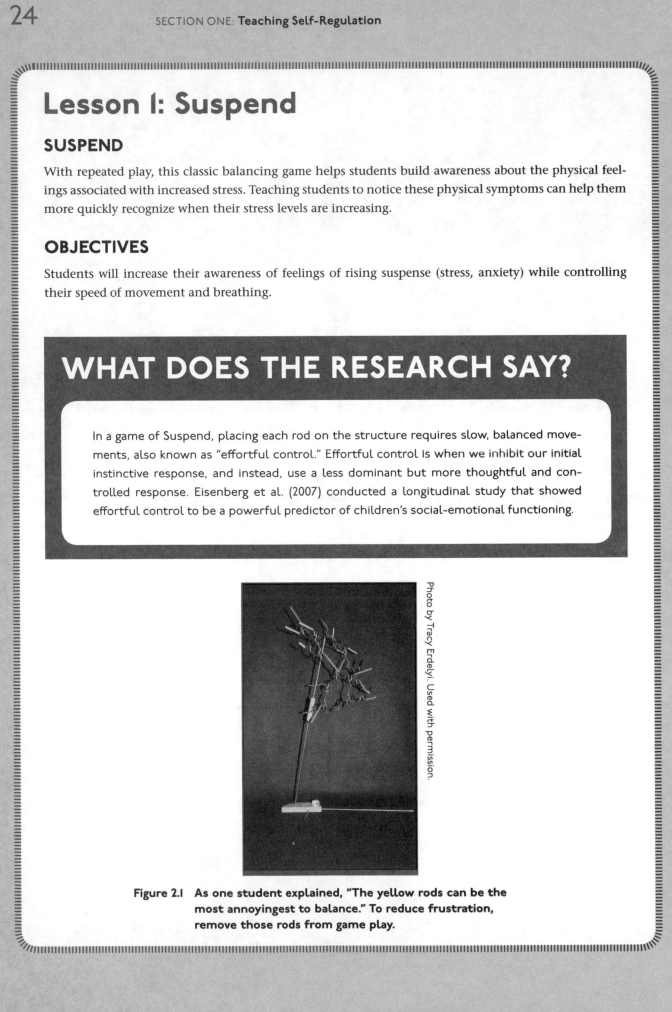

Photo by Tracy Erdelyi. Used with permission.

Figure 2.I   As one student explained, "The yellow rods can be the most annoyingest to balance." To reduce frustration, remove those rods from game play.

MATERIALS

- Suspend game (Melissa & Doug)

DIRECTIONS (FOR TWO TO SIX PLAYERS; MORE PLAYERS MAY RESULT IN TOO MUCH WAIT TIME)

This balancing game offers several options for play. For the purposes of this lesson, the following directions work well:

1. Assemble the stand.

2. Show students the die with six different colors and the corresponding color rods. Place the rods in a pile in the center.

3. Explain that a rod can only be placed on an empty hook and that the rod must match the color rolled on the die.

4. Suggest a challenge: The goal for the group is to get all the rods hanging on the structure.

5. Players take turns rolling the die and placing the corresponding color rod on the stand. If the rod falls, encourage students to keep trying.

6. Play continues around the group.

TALK ABOUT IT

It is important for the teacher to narrate the game and engage students in discussing the feelings they have as they play. Examples of questions and statements to use:

- Did you notice you were holding your breath?

- How did it feel trying to balance that rod on the stand?

- Notice how slow and controlled you need your hand to be to place the rod.

- What does that increased feeling of suspense feel like in your body?

- How does it work out for you to keep your body calm and slow down when you are feeling an increased sense of stress?

- Look how many rods we've balanced by controlling our bodies and breathing!

It may also be necessary to help students who have difficulty controlling movement and breathing when stressed. In this case, the teacher might say, "Hold the rod with me; let's place it together. Notice how slowly we have to move when we let the rod go."

FEEDBACK, ASSESSMENT, AND PRACTICE

There is a naturalistic immediate feedback in this game when the rods either maintain balance on the structure or fall. If time allows when the rods fall, encourage students to keep playing and try again for as many rods as they can place as a group. Teachers can assess through observation which students exhibit more challenges with controlling breathing and movement and who can label the physical feelings of increased stress.

(Continued)

(Continued)

TEACHING FOR GENERALIZATION

To begin generalizing these skills, students should play other games that also require them to control movement and breathing while experiencing heightened stress. Examples in this book include Suspend (pp. 24–26) and Tenzi (pp. 29–32). Once students gain practice with game play, along with associated vocabulary and verbal mediation, they can begin to describe other situations in which they experience increased stress but have a better outcome when they calm their breathing and bodies.

Lesson 2: Taboo

TABOO

This game offers a fun, fast-paced way to practice the same skills that can help students control the impulse to interrupt or blurt out in class.

OBJECTIVES

Students will increase their ability to inhibit verbal impulses. Students will increase their knowledge of categories and related topics to improve gestalt processing skills.

WHAT DOES THE RESEARCH SAY?

The process of providing verbal clues while avoiding an identified set of words (as in the game Taboo) requires students to use "inhibitory control" or the ability to use attention and reasoning to develop a response to a stimulus rather than using a habitual or impulsive response. Inhibitory control is a core executive function and is therefore trainable and improves with practice (Diamond, 2013).

MATERIALS

- Taboo game (Hasbro)

Note: *The classic version of Taboo has five "forbidden" words on each card. Taboo: Kids vs. Parents (for 8+) has only two forbidden words on each card and may provide a more appropriate place to start for some students.*

DIRECTIONS (FOR FOUR OR MORE PLAYERS, PLUS "ARBITER")

This game is most effective in achieving the objective when played according to the original directions included with Taboo. However, the directions are easily modified for use with as few as three players, with one partner giving clues to another and one "arbiter" viewing the clue giver's card to notice if any "forbidden" words are accidentally used.

1. Each player or team takes turns looking at a card from the pile and giving clues to get the other team members (or other single player) to say the "clue word" at the top of the card.

2. The clue giver is not allowed to say any word (or any part of the words) on the card, including the clue word at the top. In the rules of the game, doing so results in the card being discarded (and the turn being over). However, to avoid penalizing students at the start, it is helpful to

(Continued)

(Continued)

offer them a pass when this happens. For example, say, "We're not supposed to say any of the words on the card, but if you slip up, we're going to give you a pass."

3. A timer may be used to allow players to give as many clues as possible and elicit the correct word within the allotted time.

a. In team play, clue givers are giving clues to their own team. The team scores a point for every correct word.

b. In individual play, clue givers can amass points by every card that is correctly guessed by the other player.

TALK ABOUT IT

Success in this game requires the clue giver to inhibit the natural tendency to use the most commonly related terms associated with the clue word. To assist students in being mindful of the "forbidden words" listed on the cards, talk with them during play about strategies to avoid saying the words on the cards—for example, use self-talk as a reminder to "keep it in your thinking bubble, not in your talking bubble." For some students, it can be helpful to play this game in stages:

1. Begin by having players read aloud all the "forbidden" words and having the other player(s) guess the clue word.

2. On a subsequent round, say: "This time, try not to say the words on the card. Instead, say a bunch of other words that help your team guess the clue word."

FEEDBACK, ASSESSMENT, AND PRACTICE

Feedback for this lesson should be immediate and in the moment, with the arbiter noticing if a forbidden word has been used. Teachers and classmates can offer praise and positive social commentary each time a clue giver successfully gives clues without saying forbidden words. To assess progress, teachers may observe the number of times students can successfully avoid using a forbidden word (inhibiting verbal impulse). For example, successful inhibition on three out of six cards could be recorded at 50 percent, with data collection over time and with repetition showing the student's growth with this skill.

TEACHING FOR GENERALIZATION

During classroom conversations, teachers can encourage students to use vocabulary that is related to their topic, without first identifying the topic, to allow others to guess the topic. In upper grades, students can write their own multiple choice questions for tests (history, science, literacy, nearly any topic area!), for which they need to use the same skill of providing information that leads to one correct answer but does not reveal the answer in the choices.

Lesson 3: Tenzi

TENZI

This game can easily be played in less than a minute, making it a perfect choice when there are a few minutes for a "free-time" activity.

OBJECTIVES

Students will increase their control of speed and movement while experiencing pressure to complete a task. Students will increase their awareness of how motor control is important when experiencing stress.

WHAT DOES THE RESEARCH SAY?

Playing Tenzi based on the directions provided in this lesson plan requires that students shift their movements from "fast as possible" to "slow and steady." Practicing this shift in movement speed aids motor development. Motor development, along with interactive behavior (such as what happens when playing a game) supports the development of executive functions—the cognitive skills needed for conscious control of behavior (Koziol & Lutz, 2013).

MATERIALS

- Tenzi game (Carma Games; or set of ten dice per student)

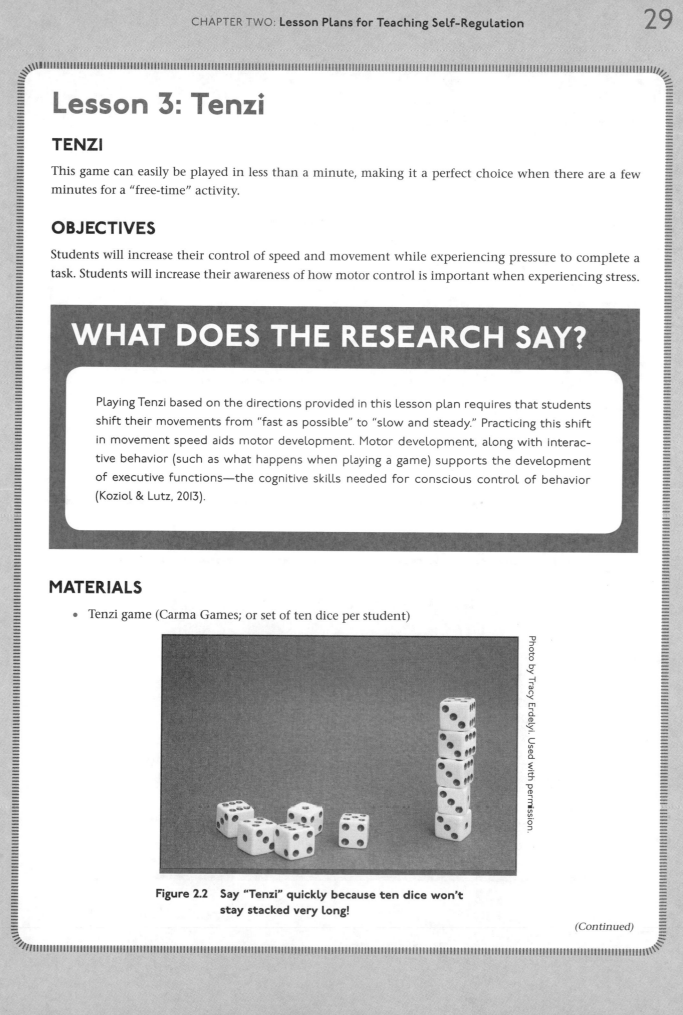

Photo by Tracy Erdelyi. Used with permission.

Figure 2.2   Say "Tenzi" quickly because ten dice won't stay stacked very long!

(Continued)

(Continued)

DIRECTIONS (FOR TWO OR MORE PLAYERS)

There are dozens of ways to play Tenzi. For the purpose of highlighting the changes in speed and body control used under pressure, start with Variation 1, below, then progress to Variation 2.

VARIATION 1

1. Each student has ten dice.

2. All students begin rolling their dice at the same time with the objective of being the first to match ten of the same number.

   Example: A player rolls the dice. Three dice land on 5. The player places those dice to the side, then continues rolling the remaining dice. With each roll, the player places matching dice to the side, attempting to be the first player to get ten of the same number.

3. The first player to get all ten dice with the same number announces "Tenzi!"

VARIATION 2

1. Each player has ten dice.

2. All players begin rolling their dice at the same time, with the objective of being the first to match ten of the same number. In this version, players stack the dice in a single column. This is tough, but some students enjoy the challenge.

   Example: A player rolls the dice (all ten) and gets two 6s. The player stacks the two matching dice, then rolls the remaining dice. As additional dice come up with 6, the player adds them to the stack. This continues until one player matches and stacks all ten dice.

3. The first player to stack all ten dice (without tipping them over) announces "Tenzi!" If a player's stacked dice fall over during the game, the player starts from the beginning.

TIP

To simplify Variation I or 2: If stacking the dice in a single column is too challenging or frustrating for students, substitute a "pyramid" formation, with students stacking the matching dice in four rows as follows:

Row I (bottom): four dice

Row 2: three dice

Row 3: two dice

Row 4 (top): one die

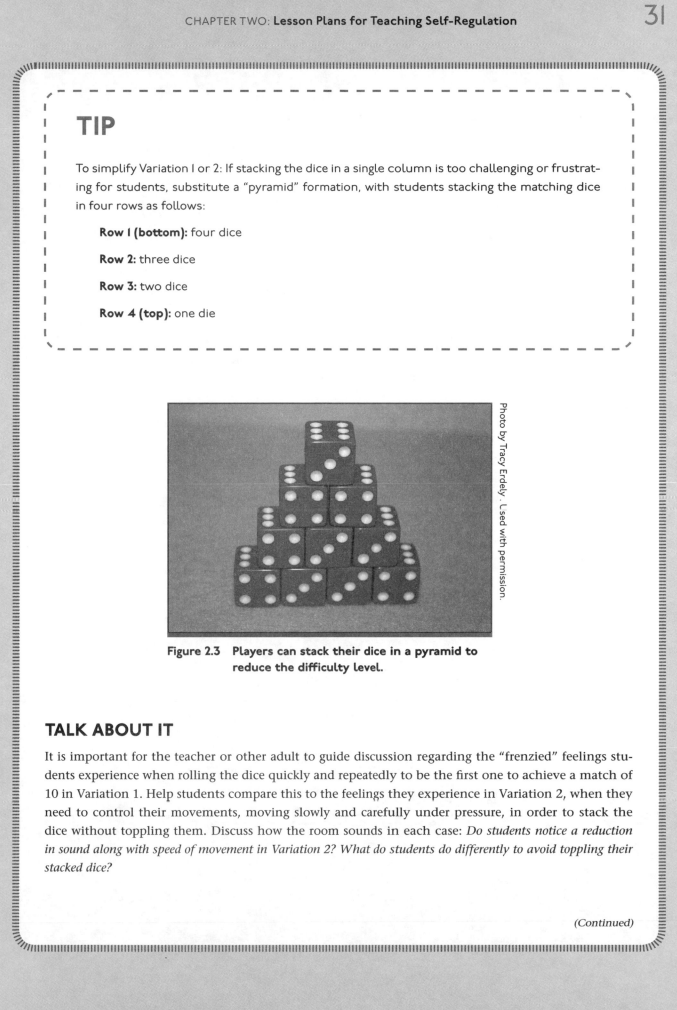

Photo by Tracy Erdely. Used with permission.

Figure 2.3   Players can stack their dice in a pyramid to reduce the difficulty level.

TALK ABOUT IT

It is important for the teacher or other adult to guide discussion regarding the "frenzied" feelings students experience when rolling the dice quickly and repeatedly to be the first one to achieve a match of 10 in Variation 1. Help students compare this to the feelings they experience in Variation 2, when they need to control their movements, moving slowly and carefully under pressure, in order to stack the dice without toppling them. Discuss how the room sounds in each case: *Do students notice a reduction in sound along with speed of movement in Variation 2? What do students do differently to avoid toppling their stacked dice?*

(Continued)

(Continued)

FEEDBACK, ASSESSMENT, AND PRACTICE

There is a considerable amount of both luck and probability involved in determining which student is the first to get to ten matched dice, and motor skill should be praised at all levels. Therefore, assessment should include the teacher's observation of students' abilities to shift their physical activity from frenzied and fast to slow and controlled.

TEACHING FOR GENERALIZATION

Continue to play Tenzi, using any of the variations included with the game, to promote awareness and control of speed and movement. Play other games as well that call for varied motor speed and control to promote generalization of these skills, such as Red Light, Green Light. Refer students back to the feelings they experienced in Tenzi when rolling and stacking the dice and the success they had when changing motor speed to meet the demands of the situation. (See Talk About It.) Ideally, this language transfers to practical, everyday examples, such as running in the gym or on the playground and walking in the hallway or classroom.

Lesson 4: Chill Out

CHILL OUT

This twist on the familiar game Go Fish helps students develop a habit of integrating an optimistic outlook into their daily lives.

OBJECTIVES

Students will learn and practice positive self-talk through multiple repetitions of self-talk statements.

WHAT DOES THE RESEARCH SAY?

Positive self-talk is a cognitive strategy that is proven to enhance performance. Many researchers have examined the relationship between positive self-talk and athletic performance, while Neck and Manz (1992) describe the influence of positive self-talk on individual and organizational performance. Reyes et al. (2015) found that users of positive self-talk experience less negative affect during anger-inducing events.

MATERIALS

- Chill Out Game Cards (Figure 2.4, p. 127–128)

DIRECTIONS (FOR TWO OR MORE PLAYERS; BEST NOT TO EXCEED SIX PLAYERS)

This game follows the basic rules for the traditional card game Go Fish.

1. Deal seven cards facedown to each player. Players remove any two-card matches in their hands and place them faceup on the table.

(Continued)

(Continued)

I can take 3 deep breaths before saying/doing anything else.	Keep trying!
Accept and move on.	I can just wait. I can handle this problem in a little while.
I can defeat this problem without crying.	I can tense up and relax my muscles to help my body feel calm.
This moment will pass.	I need some help, please.

Figure 2.4   Chill Out Game Cards

2. Players take turns asking one other player (identified by name) for a card that will make a match with a card in their hand: "(Julie), do you have _____?" (Students add the statement on the card they want.)

Example:

"Julie, do you have 'My parents or my teacher will help me if I ask?'" or "Julie, do you have 'Even hard work is easier with a calm brain?'"

TALK ABOUT IT

In this game, feedback from students is crucial to learning. Ask questions to elicit feedback, like the following examples:

- Are any of the statements on these cards new to you?
- Are any of these statements familiar?
- Which of these statements do you like/ dislike? Why?
- Are there any statements that you already tell yourself?

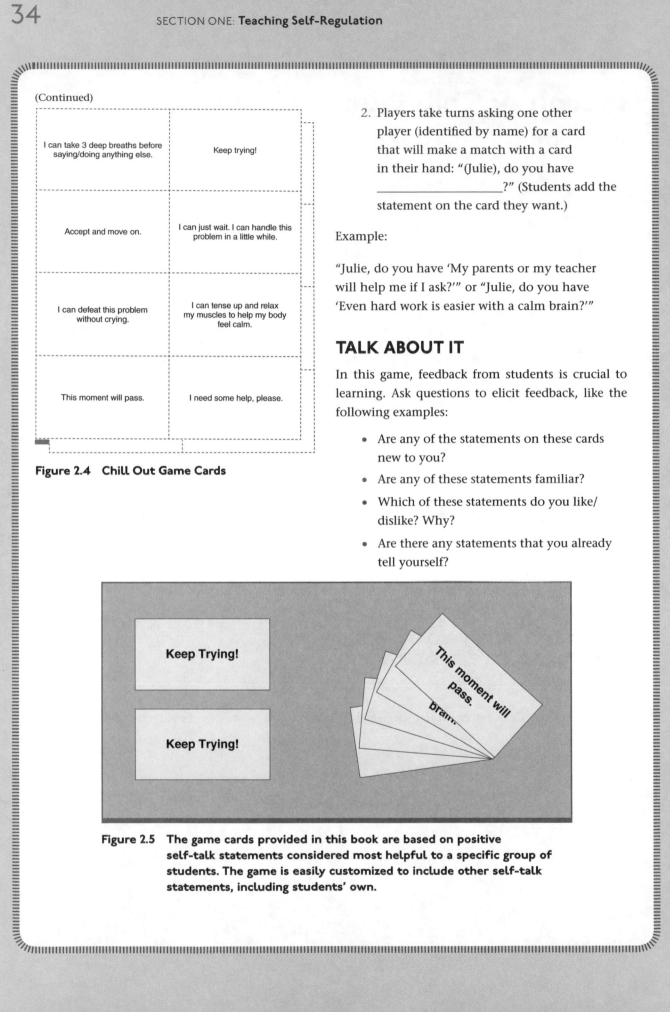

Figure 2.5   The game cards provided in this book are based on positive self-talk statements considered most helpful to a specific group of students. The game is easily customized to include other self-talk statements, including students' own.

- Which statement could you see yourself using when you are experiencing a challenging moment, such as having trouble with your homework or having a problem with a friend?

- What are some other statements you can think of that might help in a challenging situation?

FEEDBACK, ASSESSMENT, AND PRACTICE

Teachers can assess learning by observing students persisting through challenges that have previously caused escalations or shutdowns and reviewing with students positive self-talk statements they are using. Students can practice using positive self-talk statements through continued game play. As a variation, use the cards to play a Memory version of the game, following the standard directions. As students read aloud the statements on each card they turn over, they are getting the repetition they need to remember the statements and use them in other situations.

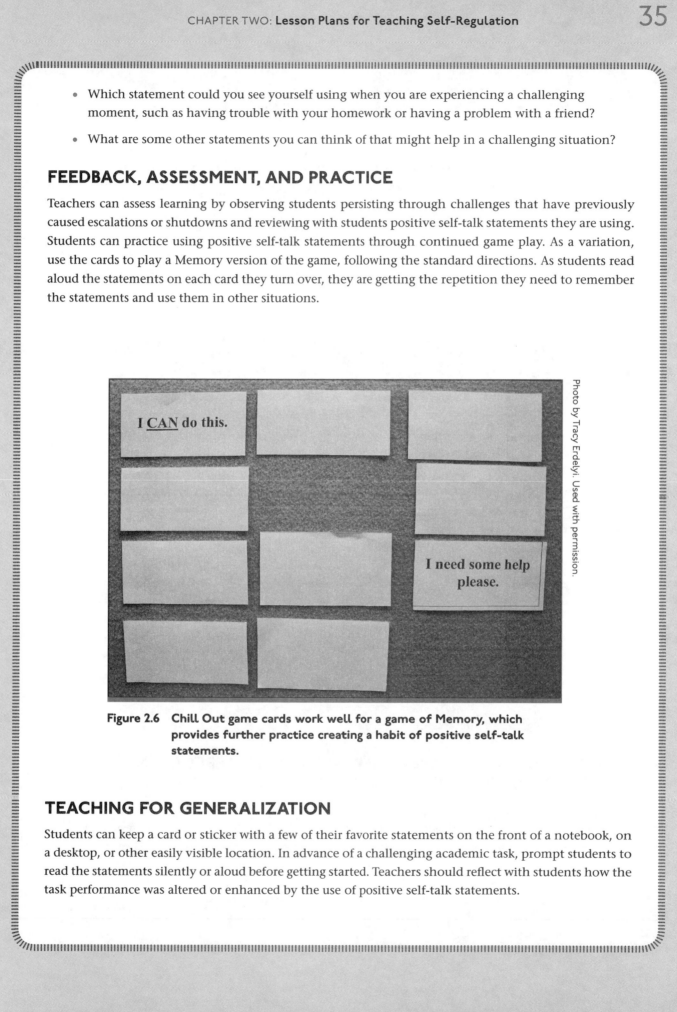

Photo by Tracy Erdelyi. Used with permission.

Figure 2.6   **Chill Out game cards work well for a game of Memory, which provides further practice creating a habit of positive self-talk statements.**

TEACHING FOR GENERALIZATION

Students can keep a card or sticker with a few of their favorite statements on the front of a notebook, on a desktop, or other easily visible location. In advance of a challenging academic task, prompt students to read the statements silently or aloud before getting started. Teachers should reflect with students how the task performance was altered or enhanced by the use of positive self-talk statements.

Lesson 5: Flexibility Points

FLEXIBILITY POINTS

There is lifelong value in learning how to handle frustration and disappointment. This activity provides practice in managing these common emotions to help students learn how to handle those times when things don't go their way—whether in a game of Sorry or with a grade in school.

OBJECTIVES

Students will reduce rigid, "single-minded" thinking and practice shifting from frustration or disappointment to acceptance and "moving on."

WHAT DOES THE RESEARCH SAY?

Accepting setbacks and persevering toward a goal is an exercise in delaying gratification, or waiting. Researchers refer to this skill as "delay ability," and it is a skill that is a proven predictor of cognitive and self-regulatory competencies in adolescence and adult life (Shoda, Mischel, & Peake, 1990). In this activity, students gain points for accepting disappointment, persevering, and waiting. Earning points can lead to a sense of accomplishment or pride—an emotional experience that is linked to improved delay ability (Willis, 2016).

MATERIALS

- Any game that includes frequent setbacks or unexpected changes for players, such as Sorry or Uno

- Flexibility Points Visual (Figure 2.7, p. 129)

DIRECTIONS (THE NUMBER OF PLAYERS WILL DEPEND ON THE PARTICULAR GAME THIS ACTIVITY IS USED WITH)

1. Introduce the game you are going to play, such as Sorry or Uno, then explain "Flexibility Points." For example, say, "We are going to play [game], but this time, there's a twist. We're going to see who can collect the most flexibility points during the game." Explain that players earn

flexibility points when they complete the following process (see Figure 2.7, Flexibility Points Visual, right):

   a. Feel disappointed or frustrated.

   b. Say, "Oh well," "Maybe next time," or "Maybe later."

   c. Move on.

2. Players earn one flexibility point each time they follow all three steps above during play. Points are not awarded for partial performance.

3. Prompt when a flexibility point can be earned. For example, when playing Sorry, say, "Oh, you just got sent back to your starting place. This is an opportunity to earn a flexibility point." The student can then say, "Oh well" and resume play, and the teacher can praise the earned flexibility point.

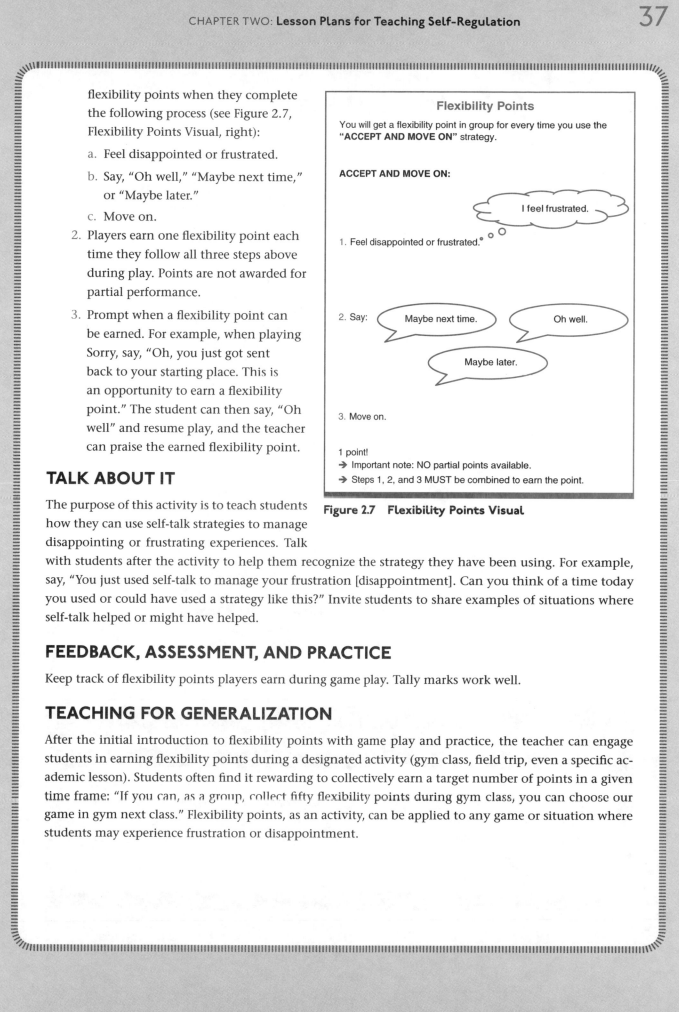

Figure 2.7 Flexibility Points Visual

TALK ABOUT IT

The purpose of this activity is to teach students how they can use self-talk strategies to manage disappointing or frustrating experiences. Talk with students after the activity to help them recognize the strategy they have been using. For example, say, "You just used self-talk to manage your frustration [disappointment]. Can you think of a time today you used or could have used a strategy like this?" Invite students to share examples of situations where self-talk helped or might have helped.

FEEDBACK, ASSESSMENT, AND PRACTICE

Keep track of flexibility points players earn during game play. Tally marks work well.

TEACHING FOR GENERALIZATION

After the initial introduction to flexibility points with game play and practice, the teacher can engage students in earning flexibility points during a designated activity (gym class, field trip, even a specific academic lesson). Students often find it rewarding to collectively earn a target number of points in a given time frame: "If you can, as a group, collect fifty flexibility points during gym class, you can choose our game in gym next class." Flexibility points, as an activity, can be applied to any game or situation where students may experience frustration or disappointment.

Lesson 6: Balloon Release

BALLOON RELEASE

This activity offers a visual way to increase awareness of preoccupying thoughts.

OBJECTIVES

Students will practice "letting go" of thoughts.

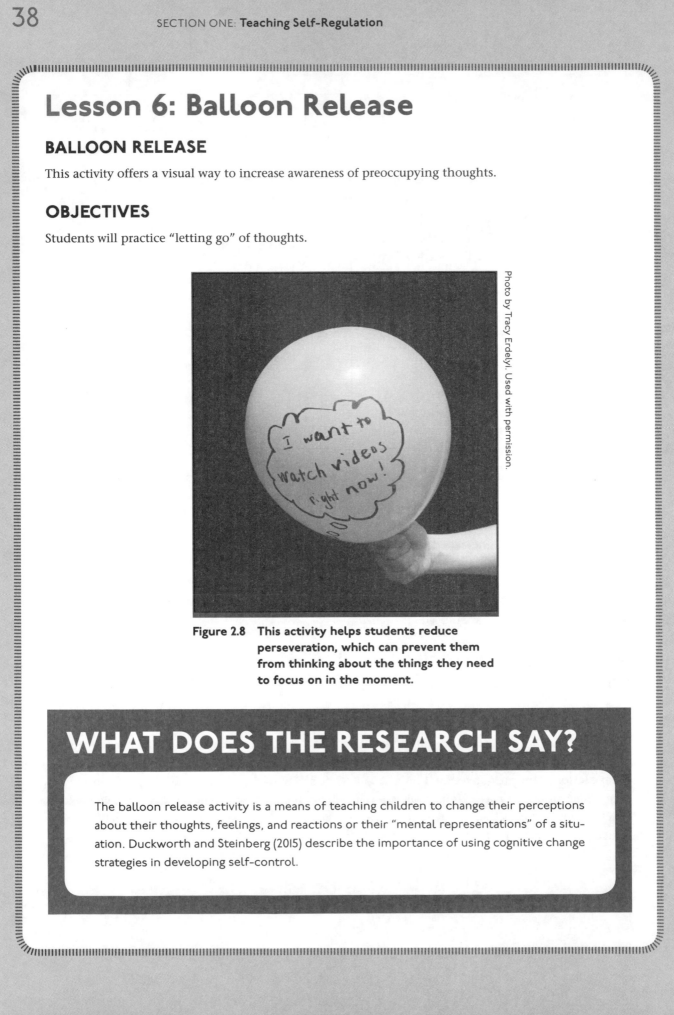

Photo by Tracy Erdelyi. Used with permission.

Figure 2.8   This activity helps students reduce perseveration, which can prevent them from thinking about the things they need to focus on in the moment.

WHAT DOES THE RESEARCH SAY?

The balloon release activity is a means of teaching children to change their perceptions about their thoughts, feelings, and reactions or their "mental representations" of a situation. Duckworth and Steinberg (2015) describe the importance of using cognitive change strategies in developing self-control.

MATERIALS

- Large latex balloon (It is helpful to have one that blows up to about the same size or a little larger than a person's head; a 16-inch balloon is a good size.)

- Permanent marker

DIRECTIONS (FOR INDIVIDUAL STUDENTS)

1. Identify a thought that a student or group of students appears to be "stuck" on, such as "I need to win," "I need to go first," or "I need to be the line leader."

2. Blow up the balloon to nearly maximum size and pinch the end of the balloon with fingers (without tying the balloon). Say to the student(s), *"Think about this balloon as a thought bubble. If you had a thought this big inside your head, it would not leave much room for other thoughts!"*

   (Another option is to guide a question and answer session with the student(s) to get at the same concept.)

3. Using the marker, draw a thought bubble on the balloon, then write or draw the thought inside it. For example, if a student is preoccupied with a video game, write the name of the game in the thought bubble and/or draw a game controller or monitor.

4. Say to student(s), *"When your thought bubble is filled with this thought, there is not enough room for other thoughts that your brain needs to be thinking about. However, your brain is flexible and can let thoughts go."*

5. Let the balloon go. It flies quickly away, making a noise that usually results in laughter from students.

6. Say to student(s), *"Now try to let go of the big thoughts that are getting in your way, and let your brain have thoughts about other things."*

TALK ABOUT IT

This activity can be used in multiple ways. If the type of thought students are having is negatively pre-occupying, the method described above can illustrate letting the thought go completely. However, if the type of thought is positive but students are preoccupied with it, the teacher can modify Step 6 (letting the balloon go) to release most of the air from the balloon and then tie the end shut.

This demonstrates hanging on to thoughts that create calm, happy, or positive feelings but keeping them "small" enough to allow for thoughts about other important things to occur at the same time. With this approach, the size of the thought bubble drawn on the balloon becomes very small. Talk with students about how the balloon can serve as a visual reminder to keep the size of that particular thought small

(Continued)

(Continued)

FEEDBACK, ASSESSMENT, AND PRACTICE

The feedback for this activity is embedded in conversation during the activity. Teachers can assess effectiveness by observing students shifting their focus away from troubling or preoccupying thoughts and on to productive, topic-related thinking.

TEACHING FOR GENERALIZATION

Once students have experienced this activity about changing their thinking, they can begin to use the process without a balloon. If other visual representation is needed, try drawing thought bubbles on a sheet of paper or a whiteboard. As a variation, use cartoon panels, with thought bubbles decreasing in size. Or try drawing desired thoughts in varying larger sizes as needed for a given situation.

Lesson 7: Uno

UNO

This classic card game comes with plenty of built-in twists and turns to provide repeated practice with executive function skills such as attentional control.

OBJECTIVES

Students will increase understanding that change happens frequently, and situations that may appear to put them at a disadvantage can actually be turned to an advantage.

WHAT DOES THE RESEARCH SAY?

When students play Uno, they are constantly shifting their attention between the most recently played card (which sets the "rules" for which card they may play next) and their hand of cards, (which determines which cards they have available to play). In addition, they must attend to directional shifts in the game, such as reversal of the order of play or skipping a player's turn. Attention shifting is one part of the executive functions that aid in self-regulation (Diamond & Lee, 2011).

MATERIALS

- Uno game (Mattel)

DIRECTIONS (FOR TWO TO TEN PLAYERS)

The directions included in this game can be followed as written for the purposes of this activity.

TALK ABOUT IT

This game requires players to understand that nothing is certain. The Buddhist teaching that "everything changes all the time" is well represented in this game. Players think they know what the assigned color is, for example, and the next player can change that status in an instant. The changes can be made by number, color, direction of play, even skipping players or requiring them to draw more cards.

The goal of the game is to be the first player to get rid of the entire hand of cards. While it may appear to be a disadvantage to have to draw many cards, as can happen throughout the game, once players have amassed a large number of cards, they can play a card at every turn and not have to draw for quite a

(Continued)

(Continued)

while. The status of "losing" or having the most cards can quickly shift to being an advantage that results in winning. Conversations with students can explore this concept: *"What were you thinking when you had so many cards? Were you thinking you were losing? Did that turn out to be true?"*

FEEDBACK, ASSESSMENT, AND PRACTICE

Throughout the game play, the teacher can verbally describe the frequent shifting from disadvantaged status to advantaged status as students experience this. The teacher can then observe students recognizing this shift for themselves during game play.

TEACHING FOR GENERALIZATION

Students can play other games, such as Sorry or I Doubt It, in which their "winning or losing" status can change frequently. Identify other times when students might experience the same feelings as in the game during academic tasks. For example, just because a student struggles with the first word or two on a spelling test does not mean that all the words on the test will be difficult. Maintaining the belief that things will work out—even when things don't appear to be going well—helps build perseverance, which increases the chance for hoped for results.

Lesson 8: Personal Space Role-Play

PERSONAL SPACE ROLE-PLAY

Repeat this activity often to help children understand the concept of personal space, which can be an issue at many levels, especially as children get older.

OBJECTIVES

Students will practice maintaining personal space and refrain from touching others without permission.

WHAT DOES THE RESEARCH SAY?

Even when impulsive behaviors such as invading others' personal space do not negatively impact academics, there may be negative social consequences. Direct instruction and practice can help students learn to control this impulsivity, leading to better interpersonal interactions. Tsukayama, Duckworth, and Kim (2013) note that it is important to distinguish between types of impulsive behaviors when developing strategies to address impulsivity.

MATERIALS

- No materials needed

DIRECTIONS (FOR SMALL GROUP OR WHOLE CLASS)

1. Discuss personal space with students and the importance of maintaining personal space and not touching others without permission.

2. Ask: "What can we do to prevent invading others' personal space when we feel the impulse to get too close or touch someone else?" Explain that practice helps.

3. Invite a student (or adult) to help model what practicing will look like: "I am going to pretend to be almost getting into [student name]'s personal space. Then, I am going to follow these steps: STOP, take a step back, and put my hands together."

4. Then pair up children to practice. Say: "Now it is your turn. Standing with a partner, each of you take a turn practicing the demonstration we just gave."

(Continued)

(Continued)

TALK ABOUT IT

Often, teachers notice students doing things they shouldn't (such as invading personal space). Talking with students about what *not* to do is helpful, but this may not prevent repeated behaviors. Guiding students to practice through role-play helps them not only know what *to* do—it empowers them to know that they *can* do it.

FEEDBACK, ASSESSMENT, AND PRACTICE

During the role-plays, it is important for the teacher to watch and listen for all students to perform each of the three steps: STOP, take a step back, put hands together. Video recordings can be used for students to demonstrate and review.

TEACHING FOR GENERALIZATION

Once students have performed the role-play, the practice can be applied to daily situations. The teacher can prompt, "You have practiced this; show what you know." Teachers can then praise the performance of the "maintaining personal space" skill, even if it is used following an episode of invading personal space.

Lesson 9: SKIP-BO

SKIP-BO

This multi-player sequencing game is easy to learn, keeping the focus on learning and practicing the self-regulatory skills involved in playing.

OBJECTIVES

Players will increase the following self-regulatory skills: forethought and planning, problem-solving, inhibiting responses, and self-reflection.

WHAT DOES THE RESEARCH SAY?

Playing SKIP-BO engages children in using executive functioning skills, effortful control, cognitive control, and impulse control. These self-regulation skills are important to the development of social and intellectual milestones that lead to positive outcomes in academics, occupational success, and health. Nigg (2017) reviews a wealth of research further describing the importance of self-regulation.

MATERIALS

- SKIP-BO card game (Mattel)

Photo by Tracy Erdelyi. Used with permission.

Figure 2.9   If you haven't played SKIP-BO, the setup is much easier than the directions might seem.

(Continued)

(Continued)

DIRECTIONS (FOR TWO TO SIX PLAYERS)

Playing the game according to the directions provided in the box will result in students practicing the desired self-regulatory skills.

TALK ABOUT IT

While students are playing, it is important to verbally mediate the use of self-regulatory skills as the students either use or fail to use them. For example, when students have a card in their stockpile that matches a card in their hand, say, "Remember that you are trying to get rid of the cards in your stockpile, and the cards in your hand are only used to help you get rid of that pile."

Label self-regulatory skills as students use them to help them recognize types of thoughts they are using to self-regulate: "I noticed you played the card from your stockpile instead of the card in your hand. Nice job resisting that impulse to play from your hand. You inhibited that response!" Or: "Oh no! You played the card from your hand and then realized you should have played from your stockpile. That thought you had when you realized your mistake is called self-reflection. Self-reflection can help you remember to avoid those mistakes in the future."

FEEDBACK, ASSESSMENT, AND PRACTICE

The process used in playing this game requires players to attend to multiple sets of cards while trying to get rid of their stockpile of cards. To achieve this goal, players may use the cards in their hand and the cards in their discard pile(s)—or both—to achieve the goal of getting rid of their stockpile. Frequently, this requires resisting the impulse to play a card from their hand when they could use a card in their stockpile instead. To succeed in this game, a player must use many self-regulatory skills, including forethought and planning, problem-solving, inhibiting responses, and self-reflection.

For assessment purposes, observe when students are using or increasing use of their forethought, planning, problem-solving, inhibitory control, and self-reflective skills. Notice which skills may require more support and prompt the use of those skills.

TEACHING FOR GENERALIZATION

The skills students use in this game transfer to activities of daily living, classroom learning, work environments, essentially all aspects of life. Once students have played the game and are familiar with the vocabulary, they can begin to label skills they are using in other activities. For example, a student who independently takes out a sheet of paper and a pencil and removes other materials from the desk in preparation for a spelling test is using forethought and planning. Encouraging students to recognize when they are using these skills can help them develop positive habits around self-regulation.

Lesson 10: Spit

SPIT

There is no turn-taking in this card game. Players move as quickly as they can from start to finish, staying alert all the while.

OBJECTIVES

Students will rapidly shift their thinking between their own cards, their opponent's cards, and the cards in between them, as a means of practicing and improving joint attention skills and flexible thinking.

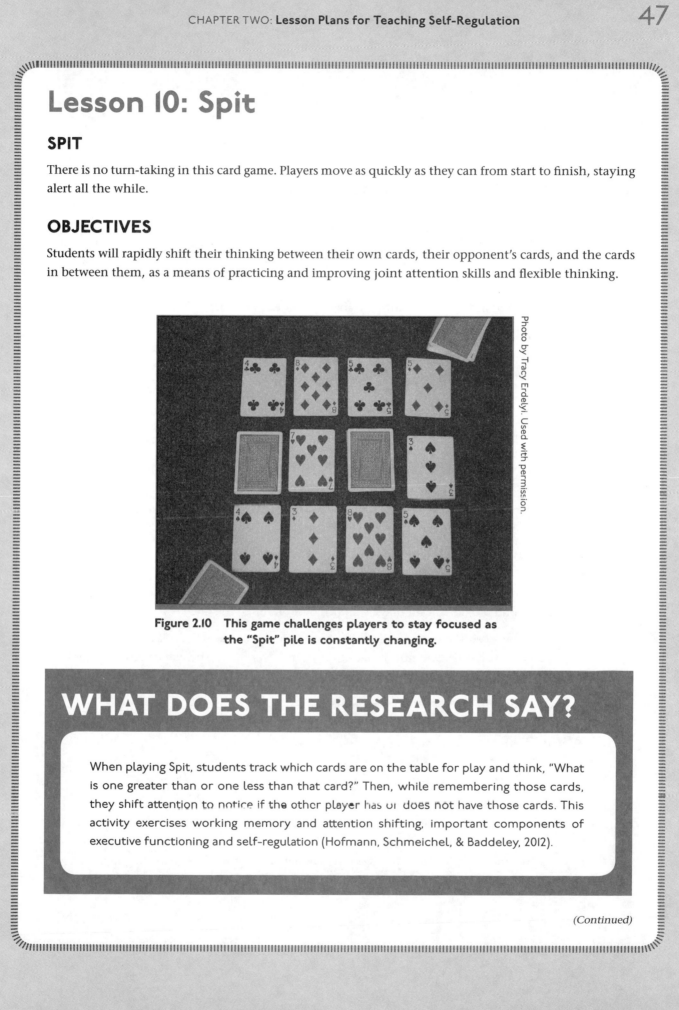

Photo by Tracy Erdelyi. Used with permission.

Figure 2.10 This game challenges players to stay focused as the "Spit" pile is constantly changing.

WHAT DOES THE RESEARCH SAY?

When playing Spit, students track which cards are on the table for play and think, "What is one greater than or one less than that card?" Then, while remembering those cards, they shift attention to notice if the other player has or does not have those cards. This activity exercises working memory and attention shifting, important components of executive functioning and self-regulation (Hofmann, Schmeichel, & Baddeley, 2012).

(Continued)

(Continued)

MATERIALS

- Deck of cards (standard)

DIRECTIONS (FOR TWO PLAYERS)

1. Divide the entire deck of cards equally between the two players.

2. Each player places two cards in the center (between the players), with one card faceup. The players decide how to start the game at the same time. Traditionally, one of them announces, "Spit," signaling the start of game play.

3. Both players then flip over four cards, placing them faceup in a row in front of them. (See photo, p. 47.)

4. Without taking turns, players simultaneously try to play the four faceup cards onto the cards that are faceup in the center. There are two faceup cards in the center to start: Both players can play on both cards. To play a card, it must be one higher or one lower than the card on top of the pile. Once a player has played a card, it becomes the new faceup card.

   Examples:

   o A player could play either a 7 or 9 on an 8.

   o A player could play either a 10 or queen on a jack.

5. As soon as players have played a card from their own four faceup cards, they replace it with another card from their deck.

6. When players get to a point where neither can play a card (none of a player's four faceup cards can be played on either center pile), they each turn over one of the facedown cards in the center, placing it on top of the two faceup piles. If neither player can play off of the new faceup cards, the second facedown card may be flipped over on top of the pile(s).

7. When all of the facedown cards in the center have been used and neither player can play a card, flip both stacks over (they will now be facedown). Turn over the top card of each stack and place it faceup. Note that there is no need to shuffle the stacks of cards being turned over.

8. Play continues until one player is out of cards.

TALK ABOUT IT

With practice, this game can be played very rapidly. Students should be paired with others of a similar experience level so that one player is not playing dramatically slower (or faster) than the other. Pairing two novices or two experienced players works best to allow students to get the most enjoyment out of the game. One of the skills players need in this game is the ability to shift attention between their cards and the other player's cards. This game is a good opportunity for experience sharing: *Were you able to focus on your cards and the other player's cards? How did this help you block the other player's moves?*

FEEDBACK, ASSESSMENT, AND PRACTICE

During game play, the teacher (or other adult) can help identify when neither player can play, encouraging students to attend not only to their own cards but also to their opponent's. Observe student performance to identify when students independently and automatically attend to each other's cards. Also observe when students are independently and automatically thinking about which cards they can play, using their cognitive flexibility to recognize multiple possibilities, such as higher or lower than a faceup card.

TEACHING FOR GENERALIZATION

This game provides practice and repetition with attending to an opponent's cards and situation. Teaching for generalization should include the use of language that is applicable to working with students in any other situation: "Can you show you are thinking about [her, him, they, me]?" In addition, teachers can build on the experiences students had during game play and say, "There is more than one way to think about this. Can you think of another way?" Or, "Can you change your thinking?"

Teaching Social Communication

CHAPTER THREE

Social Communication
The Basics

The single biggest problem in communication is the illusion that it has taken place.

—George Bernard Shaw

What is social communication? At its core, all communication is social. Often, people think of communication between teachers and students or bosses and employees as formal and therefore not "social." However, all communication involves people sharing their thoughts, beliefs, emotions, intentions, and desires with each other. Communication, such as with sharing beliefs and emotions, exposes us to acceptance or rejection from others. When acceptance occurs, an emotional bond may be established, creating the foundation for a new relationship.

The rules that govern how we communicate depend on the situation and the relationship we have with our communicative partner. Relationships are dynamic. Relationship types shift and change depending on the situation, timing, environment, and cultural factors.

RELATIONSHIP TYPES

Alan Fiske (1992) originally labeled four types of relationships in his relational models theory: communal sharing, authority ranking, equality matching, market pricing. In *The Stuff of Thought: Language as a Window Into Human Nature* (2008), Steven Pinker discusses these as three relationship types: dominance, reciprocity, and communality (pp. 401–409). The following table takes a look at each of these relationship types.

Table 3.1   Social Communication: Relationship Types

Relationship Type	Definition	Examples
Authority	I say/you do	• Boss/employee • Airline staff/passengers • Police officer/citizen
Reciprocity	Give and get or give and take	• Cashier/customer • Waitstaff/patron • Student/student
Communality	Share and share alike	• Close friends • Family members • Significant other

To understand the complexities of social communication, it is necessary to examine the expected communication within each relationship type.

RELATIONSHIP TYPE: AUTHORITY

The concept that governs this relationship type can be described as "I say, you do." Examples of this type of relationship include the following:

- Police officer and citizen

- Parent and child

- Teacher and student

- Boss and employee

- Flight staff and airline passenger

There is a social expectation carried within this relationship type that the dominant partner gives directions and the conforming partner follows those directions. Questions asked by the conforming partner are expected to be for clarification about the directions and not about the value or rationale behind the directions. Consider the following scenario that demonstrates an "authority" relationship type.

Teacher: Would you start your math work now?

Student 1:   Okay. Should I start with page 27, or should I do the worksheet first? (Clarifying question)

Student 2:   Why do I need to start my math now? (Questioning the value or rationale)

When the conforming partner doesn't understand this relationship type, the consequences can be quite serious. For children in school, for example, this might include loss of privileges, office referral, or suspension. Older individuals may face job termination, loss of relationships, or in extreme cases, arrest. When a teacher asks a student to complete a task, such as in the previous scenario, the "conforming" response should be to comply with the request, since the teacher is the "authority" or dominant partner in this relationship type.

RELATIONSHIP TYPE: RECIPROCITY

Reciprocal relationships are characterized by "give and take" or "give and get." Examples of this type of relationship include the following:

- Wait staff and patron

- Therapist and client

- Healthcare provider and patient

- Passengers on an airplane

- Student and student (in a classroom)

The essential expectation in this relationship is that we each get something out of the interaction with each other. That "something" could be payment for a service or product (and, conversely, a service or product for payment) or keeping each other comfortable by following common social expectations, such as in the classroom or on an airplane. For example, when riding on an airplane, Passenger A might expect Passenger B to listen to music on headphones instead of playing music aloud. Each passenger grants the other the choice of listening so that both have the airplane experience they desire, even though in other aspects of life, they are strangers.

Serious problems can arise when a relationship type should be reciprocal but a partner does not understand or misuses the relationship boundaries. Bullying is an example of this, and again, the consequences can be significant. For example, students who are bullied may experience a decline in academic achievement, isolation, depression, and anxiety. Those who engage in bullying behavior may also experience negative outcomes, such as an increase in other risky behavior.

RELATIONSHIP TYPE: COMMUNALITY

Communality relationships are those that include family and close friends. The guideline for these relationships is that everyone has equal status and there is a "share and share alike" mentality. Within this type of relationship, people share personal information, food, personal items, even living space. Consider the communication that happens between people who have a communality relationship:

Person 1:	Are you going to finish that pasta?
Person 2:	No, do you want it?
Person 1:	Don't mind if I do!

The expectation within this relationship type is that the partners can share everything with each other and they are on equal ground when negotiating or advocating for their needs. However, when considering the differences in the styles of communication that occur in the other relationship types, we begin to see the complexities of social communication.

COMPLEXITIES OF SOCIAL COMMUNICATION

The complexity of social communication lies in the fact that these relationship types are not static. For example, a parent might tell a child, "It's time for bed." This is an example of the dominance relationship—the parent is exerting the authority to tell the child to go to bed on time. In this scenario, it's not expected that the child will say, "No, I don't feel like it." The communality relationship might be the parent asking the child, "Do you want to watch a movie with me?" and the child responding, "No, I don't feel like it." In this case, the child's response is appropriate because the relationship is being governed by communality, not authority.

As these examples show, both people in the relationship (such as parent and child) are required to identify at which times the relationship is governed by authority and compliance and which times it is governed by communality because this changes the rules for communication.

One complexity of social communication, then, is understanding the shifting and changing of relationship types and the rules that govern communication within each relationship type. Another complexity can be how we use language in ways that does not directly express what we mean. When a teacher tells a student, "This would be a good time to get started on your math," the message is really, "Start working on your math now." When parents tell their children, "It would be great if you would set the table," they mean, "Set the table now."

> To provide practice with identifying and understanding relationship types, see the Relationship Types Card Sort lesson (pp. 72–74).

As these examples show, our communication may at times be far too polite to directly convey our intent. Problems arise when the more concrete and literal thinkers of our society take a request literally, when it is actually meant as a command. In this case, the student may hear the teacher's request about it being a good time to get started on math and may even agree with the teacher and then still fail to get started.

A psychologist tells the story of working with a client, who, using a demanding tone, stated, "Give me that pencil!" The psychologist calmly tried to coach the client into using a more polite tone, saying, "Could you say that again?" We can infer that the intent was to have the client change his tone, to ask for the pencil politely. The client, however, restated, "Give me that pencil!" using the exact same demanding tone.

In the case of the student and the teacher, upon seeing the student fail to get started on math, the teacher might think that the student is confused about the math or does not want to do the assignment. The student, however, may have simply misunderstood the command as being an optional request due to misunderstanding that in this case the relationship is governed by the communication rules applying to authority and compliance and not the rules for communality. In the case of the psychologist and client, the client might honestly be complying when the command is repeated. However, the psychologist may interpret this communication as defiance.

Once this misunderstanding occurs within communicative partners, communication breaks down further. The teacher might quickly become frustrated and could soon be saying, "Why haven't you started your math yet? I have asked you repeatedly." The student, having not realized the polite requests were actually commands, now experiences more confusion and frustration and will quickly lose motivation to interact with the teacher. Direct language can help to ease the confusion. If the teacher says, "It's time to start your math" or "Start your math now," there is little opportunity to misunderstand this is a command.

Individuals who struggle with social communication often understand only one relationship type and believe that this relationship type governs communication in all relationships. They may, therefore, experience frequent confusion or frustration when interacting with others. They may also express appreciation when others use direct language with them.

Understanding shifting relationship types and direct versus indirect language are important aspects of the give-and-take exchanges in communication. As complex as these two aspects of communication are, they are only the beginning of good social communication.

NONVERBAL COMMUNICATION

It's widely reported that over 90 percent of communication is nonverbal. In the late sixties, two research studies (Mehrabian & Wiener, 1967; Mehrabian & Ferris, 1967) emerged describing the impact of verbal tone and facial expression on a communicator's message. The authors developed a formula suggesting that 55 percent of a message is conveyed through body language, 38 percent is carried through tone of voice, and only 7 percent is carried through the actual words spoken.

Author and public speaker Joe Navarro (Navarro & Karlins, 2008) has written extensively about nonverbal communication. He developed his expertise in body language during his career as an FBI investigator and currently teaches about the importance of interpreting nonverbal and paraverbal communication. Paraverbals, such as listening noises ("hmmm"), rate, pitch, and tone, all influence the meaning of a message. The change in meaning due to tone, for example, becomes quite clear when a sarcastic tone is used versus a sincere tone. Take the example of this statement: "That's a nice shirt." Said with a sincere tone, the words carry the meaning, "I truly like your shirt and think it looks great." The same words, said with a sarcastic tone, carry the meaning, "I don't like that shirt at all."

Body language includes cultural expectations when interacting with others. We may turn our faces and shoulders toward our communicative partners, which sends the message that we are attending to each other. We maintain a physical proximity expected for our culture. This may include an "arm's length" guideline so that we are not so close as to make others feel uncomfortable or so far as to make others feel we are not interested.

People who struggle with social communication often have difficulty interpreting and using nonverbal aspects of communication. They may have facial expressions that are somewhat flat or minimal changes in expression. They may have a voice tone that does not match their emotional state—playful-sounding when angry or serious-sounding when happy. Their use of body language may not accurately convey their intended meaning either. Explicit instruction and practice in the use of nonverbal communication skills may be necessary to clear up confusion in communicative exchanges.

To practice nonverbal communication with students, try Ball Toss Communication (pp. 79–80).

In addition, it is important for individuals to understand a very important format of communication that happens across all relationship types: conversation. Some very common mistakes occur when people try to teach conversation. Eye contact, conversational turn-taking, and staying on topic are all troublesome areas to teach because if practiced too explicitly, they can lead to awkward, unnatural conversations.

When people converse "in person" and one person does not make eye contact, the conversation feels uncomfortable. However, if that person is then instructed that eye contact is necessary, he or she may change to a behavior of staring, which is also uncomfortable. Instead of eye contact, we can use the term to "eye gaze." Eye gaze is used to both convey and gather information. Our eye gaze provides information to others as to what we might be thinking about and offers clues about the level of interest our communicative partner has in the interaction.

TEACHING CONVERSATION

Teaching conversation is challenging! The basic aspects of conversation—topics, questions, comments, and nonverbal elements—can all be explicitly taught. However, weaving all of the elements together so that there is a natural feeling and flow to the conversation can be quite difficult.

TEACHING METHOD

Frequently, teachers make the mistake of providing verbal directions ("Can you make a comment about that?") or eliciting a comment from each student one at a time. The latter method results in each student having a structured, guided interaction with the teacher, but it neglects teaching them how to generate spontaneous comments and questions with one another. Instead, explicit teaching about the types of questions we ask and the types of comments we make and then practice using both, results in students having success with spontaneous, natural conversation.

TYPES OF QUESTIONS AND COMMENTS

People use different types of questions and comments when conversing. Some questions, such as "What time is it?" seek precise information and don't lend themselves to a continued back and forth exchange. The following chart shows the types of questions and comments that people use in conversation. When teaching conversation skills, teachers can focus on having students develop skills with the different types of questions and comments.

Table 3.2 Types of Questions and Comments

Self-based questions	"How do you like my shirt?" These are the questions people ask to gain input from another about their own looks, ideas, experiences, and so forth.
Other-based questions	"What did you do last weekend?" These are questions that people ask to gain information about someone else.
Follow-up questions	These are the questions people ask about what someone has just said. Statement: "I baked cookies this weekend." Follow-up question: "What kind of cookies did you make?"
Related comments	These are comments that relate in some way to a portion of what someone has just said. Statement: "I baked cookies this weekend." Related comment: "I love cookies."
Unrelated comments	These comments do not relate in any way to what someone has just said. Statement: "I baked cookies this weekend." Unrelated comment: "I hope they have French fries for lunch today."
Reusable comments	"Interesting." "Tell me more about that." These are comments that a person can make in response to almost anything another person has said, regardless of the topic or content.

Self-based questions are valuable in showing others that their opinions matter, but too many of these quickly make the conversation feel one-sided and can result in the conversation coming to a premature end. Other-based questions are valuable in showing others that we care about them, and they are good conversation starters. Follow-up questions are very valuable for conversation maintenance. They can only be used in response to what someone else is talking about, so they are highly effective in making others feel that we are interested in them.

> To provide practice with increasing students' use of follow-up questions, see Follow-Up Questions (pp. 66–68).

Related comments can only be used in response to what someone else has said, so they are valuable for conversation maintenance and showing interest in others. However, they do not need to be completely about the other person's topic. For example, a conversational exchange using related comments might look like this:

Person 1:   I saw *The Secret Life of Pets* this weekend. That was a funny movie!

Person 2:   I saw that movie this weekend, too! Then we went bowling.

In this example, a related comment is used, but the topic of conversation shifts from the funny movie to another activity. This is a fine example of the way that conversational topics naturally shift, sometimes within just one conversational exchange, and it highlights the importance for teachers to avoid setting goals for students that involve the student staying on a single conversational topic for a specific number of exchanges.

Unrelated comments can be valuable to change the topic of a conversation, but when they occur in the middle of a fluid conversation, they can make people feel uncomfortable. It is important to teach students to recognize the difference between related and unrelated comments and how to specifically identify the connections between topics.

Unexpected, surprising, or rude comments sometimes happen in conversation. The goal in teaching good conversation skills includes teaching students how to avoid making these unexpected comments by increasing student understanding of how the comments make others feel.

For more information on teaching students to interpret other people's feelings, see Chapter 5, Perspective-Taking: The Basics (pp. 89–98).

Reusable comments are valuable in creating the impression that we are interested in others and allow us processing time to formulate something else to say. They are helpful when we are not sure how to respond to something that someone has just said. The drawback in using too many reusable comments is that they do not provide content input into the conversation from two or more sides.

In general, strong conversational skills involve using a blend of the different question and comment types. Often, those who struggle with conversations have difficulty understanding or formulating one or more of the question and comment types. The lesson plans for social communication that follow are designed to provide instruction on the elements of communication, as well as the development of fluid, strong, conversation skills.

The chapter that follows, "Lesson Plans for Teaching Social Communication," offers ten lesson plans for activities and games to teach communication skills, providing for the "in the moment" learning and practice children need to generalize skills in new situations. As you use these activities and games with students, keep the following tips in mind:

- It may be surprising to see how much direct practice and repetition students need with voice tone or body language.

- Students often have fun demonstrating how to say things the "wrong" way (too fast, too loud, too quiet, etc.). If they are struggling with voice tone, volume, or speed during any of the games, ask them to show the wrong way first, then change to the right way.

- Increase "wait time" when students are having difficulty generating responses, or write some response options on the board that they can use when they are having difficulty thinking of a question or a comment.

- Refer to What Does the Research Say? in each lesson to learn more about how the games and activities support the development of social communication skills, including the development of memory and the importance of critical thinking skills throughout the school years.

CHAPTER FOUR

Lesson Plans for Teaching Social Communication

Table 4.1   Social Communication Lesson Plans Overview

Game/Activity	Areas of Focus	Page
Hidden Message	Treasure hunt to collect and assemble clues	62
I Doubt It	Traditional card game using verbal and nonverbal communication	64
Follow-Up Questions	Show interest and keep the conversation going	66
Hedbanz	Ask questions and figure out answers	69
Relationship Types Card Sort	Understand relationship types	72
5-Second Rule	Categorize and answer quickly	75
Hidden Objects	Multiple meaning words, abstract thinking, and problem-solving	77
Ball Toss Communication	Conversational turn-taking	79
Word on the Street	Collaboration skills	81
Beanbag Crash	Collaboration skills	83

Lesson 1: Hidden Message

HIDDEN MESSAGE

This team-based activity encourages reciprocal communication, language interpretation, problem-solving, and gestalt processing.

OBJECTIVES

Participants will use social communication skills to give and receive directions as they search for plastic eggs that have been hidden around the room (or outdoor space). They will then use problem-solving and language-inferencing skills to assemble the strips inside the eggs into a coherent message.

WHAT DOES THE RESEARCH SAY?

Gestalt processing is an important part of social learning. Gestalt theory holds that the whole is greater than the sum of the parts. When learning happens in the context of real-life experiences rather than in separate pieces, the brain can better organize the learning as a more complete "picture." Learning social communication skills in the context of the activity Hidden Message is an example of this. Koffka (2013) offers an extensive discussion of gestalt processing and social learning in *Principles of Gestalt Psychology*.

MATERIALS

- Plastic eggs (the number will vary depending on the length of the hidden message and the number of segments the message is divided into)

- Paper

- Table, desk, or central location to collect and assemble the message strips

DIRECTIONS (FOR TWO TO SIX PLAYERS; WITH MORE THAN SIX PLAYERS, THE "PROBLEM-SOLVING AS A SMALL GROUP" ELEMENT GETS LOST)

1. Begin by writing a message on a sheet of paper.

   Sample message:

   > *We are such a great team! We found all the words to create this message. To celebrate, let's each choose a prize from the treasure chest!*

2. Then segment the message into single words or phrases. For example, divide the message into several strips with three or more words on each. Sentences can be split, but make sure the last word and ending punctuation of one sentence isn't split from the first word of the next sentence. The placement of capitalization and punctuation provide clues to assembling the message in the correct order.

3. Place each segment in a plastic egg. Then hide the eggs before participants arrive (or while they cover their eyes).

4. Players are given parameters explaining where the eggs may and may not be hidden. For example: *"All eggs are in plain view and can be seen without opening or closing anything. You might find eggs as low as floor level but no higher than the top of my head."*

5. Players then search for eggs, bringing each egg they find to a central location (without opening it and removing the strips inside).

6. Once all of the eggs have been collected, players open the eggs together and read the word and/or phrase in each. They then work together to assemble and read the message.

TALK ABOUT IT

This game provides social learning in the areas of reciprocal communication, language interpretation, problem-solving, and gestalt processing. Arguing and negotiation about placement of phrases in this game is natural. Use these moments to guide conversations about clues, such as punctuation, to help students practice problem-solving and communication. For example, say, "Look. There's a period here. What does that tell you about where this goes?"

FEEDBACK, ASSESSMENT, AND PRACTICE

Players receive immediate and naturalistic feedback both as they find eggs and as they search areas without finding eggs. Provide coaching and assistance as needed to help students find eggs and assemble the final message, maintaining a positive experience for all players. For continued practice, play the game again and again, using different messages each time.

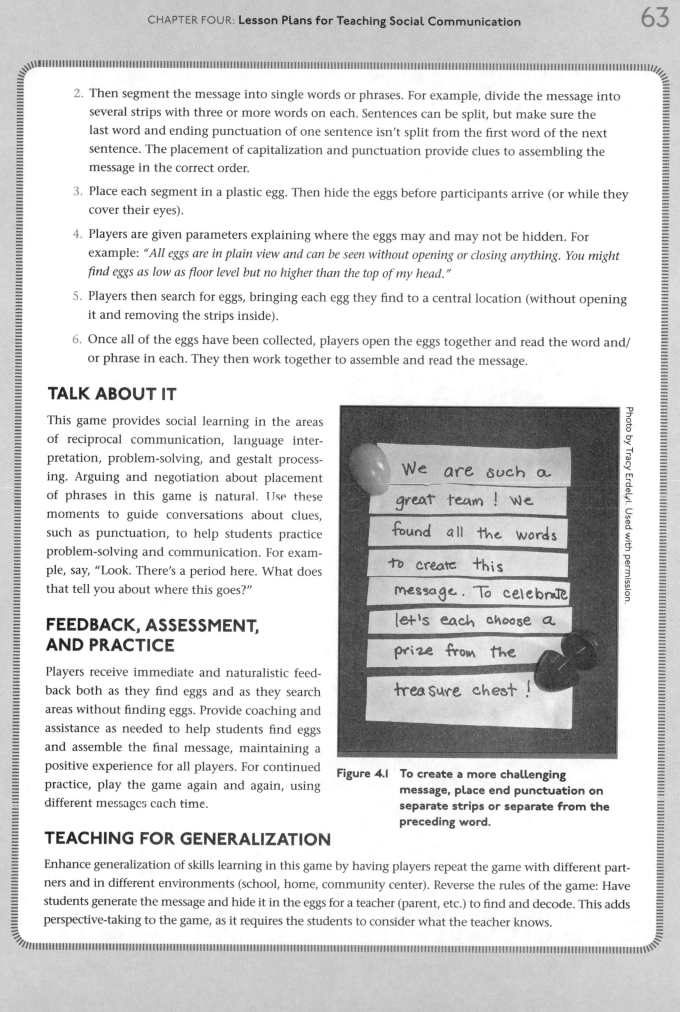

Photo by Tracy Erdelyi. Used with permission.

Figure 4.1   To create a more challenging message, place end punctuation on separate strips or separate from the preceding word.

TEACHING FOR GENERALIZATION

Enhance generalization of skills learning in this game by having players repeat the game with different partners and in different environments (school, home, community center). Reverse the rules of the game: Have students generate the message and hide it in the eggs for a teacher (parent, etc.) to find and decode. This adds perspective-taking to the game, as it requires the students to consider what the teacher knows.

Lesson 2: I Doubt It

I DOUBT IT

Players use social communication and self-regulation skills to bluff their way to a winning hand.

OBJECTIVES

Players use social communication skills to achieve the goal of being the first player to use all of the cards in their hand. Target skills include observing and accurately interpreting facial expression, body language, and voice tone, as well as using body language, voice tone, and facial expression to deliver the intended message.

WHAT DOES THE RESEARCH SAY?

Playing games such as I Doubt It promotes positive outcomes associated with self-regulation. In "The Evidence Base for How We Learn: Supporting Students' Social, Emotional, and Academic Development," Jones and Kahn (2017) report that "early self-control predicts a range of long-term outcomes, including better physical health and personal finances, and lower substance dependence and criminal activity" (p. 12).

MATERIALS

- Deck of cards (standard; remove jokers/wild cards)

DIRECTIONS (FOR TWO TO TEN PLAYERS)

Note: *This is a bluffing game, and a player can play any card while claiming it is a different card. As a card is played, another player can challenge the play by saying, "I doubt it."*

1. The dealer distributes cards until there are none left. This may leave some players with one extra card, which does not have any negative impact on the potential for winning the game (and could work as an asset in some situations). Players should be informed that it does not matter if they have the exact same number of cards.

2. The game starts with the first player placing at least one ace facedown at the center of the table, saying, "I have one [two, three, four] ace(s)." This is also an opportunity for bluffing:

   - Player 1 may not have any aces or may want to play cards that are not aces.

   - This player can bluff, playing up to four cards while stating that the cards are all aces.

3. Any player can challenge the card(s) played by saying, "I doubt it." For example, if Player 1 claims to be playing three aces but another player is holding two aces, that player might make a challenge.

4. The player being challenged turns over the cards. Players who are caught bluffing must take the entire pile from the center and add it to their hand. Players will want to understand that it is not much of a risk to bluff if you're the first player because there are not any extra cards in the pile.

5. In turn, players play cards in their hands that follow the sequence (ace, 2, 3, 4, etc.), stating how many of the particular card they have: "I have one 2 [3, 4, 5, etc.]."

6. Once the king is played, the next player must claim to be playing an ace. The game then continues with numbers starting at 2.

7. There are moments throughout the game when players may have very few cards in their hand and may not have the required card for their turn. This situation requires players to bluff and quite possibly get caught. There is no "passing" on one's turn.

8. The game continues until one player successfully plays all cards in the hand.

TALK ABOUT IT

This game primarily targets social communication skills. However, it also requires players to inhibit the impulse to state the actual cards being played when bluffing. In this way, it also integrates self-regulation skills. In addition, players must maintain focus on which card is being played by each player and plan ahead for which card will be expected for their turn. A good bluff requires the conveyance of self-confidence, which is a useful communication skill for real-life situations of uncertainty, such as giving a class presentation.

Talk with students about speaking with confidence. Demonstrate a statement that lacks confidence, and then restate the same statement with a confident tone and body language. Ask, "What are some situations you could be in when using confident communication might be important?" "Are there times when sounding confident might work against you?"

FEEDBACK, ASSESSMENT, AND PRACTICE

Players may have a difficult time bluffing. Provide coaching to help players adjust their body language, tone of voice, and facial expressions to convey the intended message. Players may also have difficulty accurately interpreting body language, voice tone, or facial expressions that signal a bluff. For example, a bluffer may use a quiet or uncertain voice, try to play the turn very quickly, or even state the actual card played instead of the designated card for the turn. Provide coaching for these errors by saying, "Try to say that using a confident voice," or "Remember to say the card you are pretending to play, not the actual card."

TEACHING FOR GENERALIZATION

To help students generalize the bluffing skill, have them play the game with new people and evaluate the effectiveness of their skills on different partners. Introduce additional conversation games such as Two Truths and a Lie, in which each person shares three pieces of information about themselves in a sincere and convincing manner. However, they are instructed to share only two true items, along with one that is false. Others then guess which item is false.

Lesson 3: Follow-Up Questions

FOLLOW-UP QUESTIONS

This activity is a motivating way to help students enhance their conversation skills—a building block for social success.

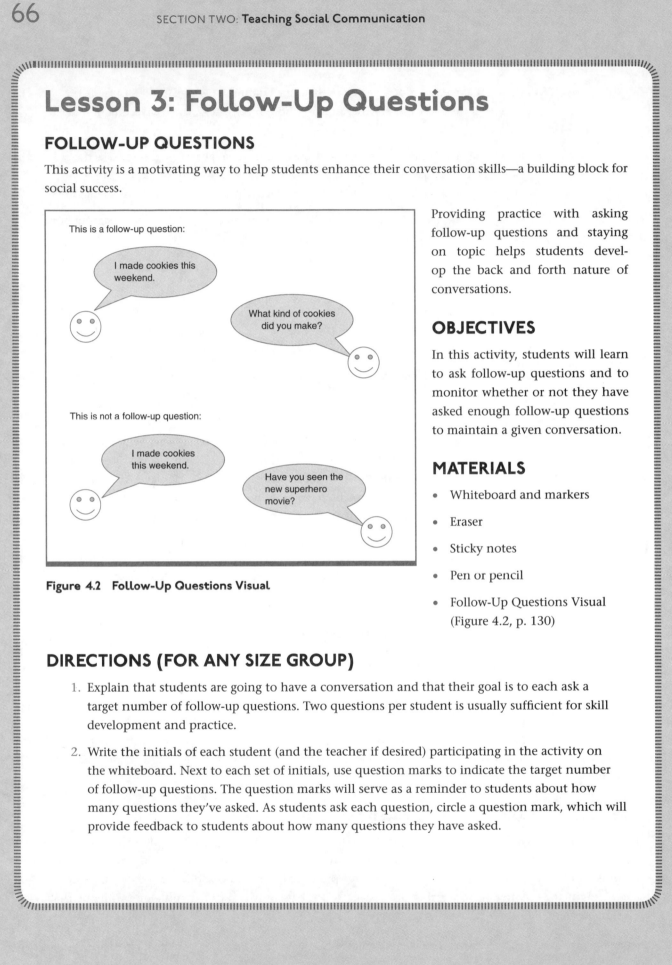

This is a follow-up question:

I made cookies this weekend.

What kind of cookies did you make?

This is not a follow-up question:

I made cookies this weekend.

Have you seen the new superhero movie?

Figure 4.2   Follow-Up Questions Visual

Providing practice with asking follow-up questions and staying on topic helps students develop the back and forth nature of conversations.

OBJECTIVES

In this activity, students will learn to ask follow-up questions and to monitor whether or not they have asked enough follow-up questions to maintain a given conversation.

MATERIALS

- Whiteboard and markers
- Eraser
- Sticky notes
- Pen or pencil
- Follow-Up Questions Visual (Figure 4.2, p. 130)

DIRECTIONS (FOR ANY SIZE GROUP)

1. Explain that students are going to have a conversation and that their goal is to each ask a target number of follow-up questions. Two questions per student is usually sufficient for skill development and practice.

2. Write the initials of each student (and the teacher if desired) participating in the activity on the whiteboard. Next to each set of initials, use question marks to indicate the target number of follow-up questions. The question marks will serve as a reminder to students about how many questions they've asked. As students ask each question, circle a question mark, which will provide feedback to students about how many questions they have asked.

WHAT DOES THE RESEARCH SAY?

Asking questions is an effective way of improving emotional intelligence, and when emotional intelligence increases, question-asking abilities also improve (Brooks & John, 2018). Of the various types of questions, Brooks and John note the "special power" of follow-up questions. Follow-up questions show attention to the content of what was said and an interest in hearing more about it.

3. Define "follow-up question" explicitly: a question you ask about something someone has just said. Write the definition and an example on the whiteboard to provide visual support for students throughout the activity.

Example:

Person 1:   I made cookies last night.

Person 2:   What kind of cookies?

JE	? ?
AW	? ?
BP	? ?
DS	? ?

Figure 4.3   Follow-Up Questions Example

4. Invite a student to start off the conversation—for example, by sharing a piece of information about the day. Once the information has been stated, another student can respond. Depending on that response, do one of the following:

- If that student replies with a follow-up question, such as in the above example, circle one of that student's question marks on the board.

- Naturally, students may also respond with comments rather than questions, such as "Yum." If no student asks a follow-up question, see methods for prompting in the Talk About It section of this lesson.

- Provide modeling by asking a follow-up question and then circling a question mark next to your own initials.

TALK ABOUT IT

A visual, partial prompt in a cloze format is ideal for students who require prompting. For example, if the informational comment was "I went on vacation," provide a prompt by writing, "Where did you _____?" on a sticky note and placing it in front of a student who is struggling to formulate a question. Listing question words (who, what, why, where, when, how, do) on the whiteboard is another helpful prompt that can provide support throughout the activity.

(Continued)

(Continued)

FEEDBACK, ASSESSMENT, AND PRACTICE

Immediate visual feedback is available to students throughout the activity since they can see when a question mark next to their initials gets circled. This allows them to see both what they have done and what they have yet to do. This visual feedback method can also serve as a record of student performance. One fast, simple way to do this is to take a photo of the whiteboard at the end of the activity.

Use this activity at least once a week to provide practice. For assessment purposes, begin by having a group conversation with students and noting on a list of student names with a plus or minus which students ask follow-up questions and which do not. After weekly practice is implemented, another conversation can be held to note which students independently use follow-up questions and which use the questions when prompted.

TEACHING FOR GENERALIZATION

Generalization can occur when the students have any opportunity for conversation outside of the structured activity. At the end of the structured activity, the teacher might say, "Please try to use at least two follow-up questions when you are talking with friends at lunch." Alternatives could include talking with the nurse, the principal, the guidance counselor, and parents. Other adults can be prepared to observe for follow-up questions.

Lesson 4: Hedbanz

HEDBANZ

This simple game of "What am I?" is easy to learn and play, making it a good one for repeated practice.

OBJECTIVES

This game facilitates skill development in asking and answering questions and in putting language details together to determine the main idea.

Photo by Tracy Erdelyi. Used with permission.

Figure 4.4   Naturally, you'll want to play this game in a room where reflections from mirrors won't give the words or pictures away!

WHAT DOES THE RESEARCH SAY?

This activity directly supports the skills students need to grow as readers, specifically to put together supporting details in order to determine the main idea. As students get older, reading tends to become more about "reading to learn" rather than "learning to read." However, adolescents who struggle with reading still need direct instruction in general reading strategies, such as finding the main idea (Faggella-Luby et al., 2012).

(Continued)

(Continued)

MATERIALS

- Hedbanz game (Spin Master)

DIRECTIONS (FOR TWO TO SIX PLAYERS)

1. The headbands that come with this game sit horizontally across each player's forehead. They are adjustable to fit any head size. There is a groove in the headband that should be aligned with the center of the player's forehead. Once each player has a headband on, place the cards in the headbands.

2. Separate the question prompt card from the picture cards. Shuffle the picture cards. Depending on the age and level of players, they could choose a card (picture-side down) from the deck and place it in their own headband, or another player, helper, or teacher could place the card for them. Care should be given to keep each player from seeing the picture on their own headband prior to playing the game.

3. Once all players have a card in their headband, they can begin asking each other questions about the item or animal pictured on their headbands. See options for turn-taking sequences under Talk About It. The first player with an accurate guess could be called the winner, but it may be more fun for all players to play until all players have correctly guessed their picture.

4. Pay special attention throughout the game to player guesses that either match or don't match clues the player has received. For more information, see Talk About It.

TALK ABOUT IT

Sequence of turns: One easy way to play this game is for each player to ask one question, receive the answer, and then pass the play to the next player. However, to emphasize skill development for finding the main idea, allow each player to ask several (four, for example) questions during one turn. This may help students keep track of the combined clues and use the relationships among the clues to guess the main idea.

There are two important pieces of feedback that the teacher must provide players throughout the game:

1. Explicit connections between how the clues match or do not match the final answer guesses.

2. Praise and positive social feedback identifying the moments when students suppress saying aloud what is pictured on each other's cards, and/or when they suppress the impulse to look at their own card prior to guessing.

Attend to guesses that do not match the clues. For example, if a player asks, "Am I alive?" in reference to the picture on the headband and the answer is "Yes," a "matching" guess might be a plant or animal. A guess that would not match that clue might be "furniture." In the case of repeated non-matching guesses, create a three-column chart (see Figure 4.5) for students to track clues, guesses, and notes.

Clues	Guesses	Notes
Alive	—	—
Not taller than me	Ice cream?	Doesn't match clues
Furry	Cat?	Matches clues but not correct
Pet	Dog?	Matches clues and correct

Figure 4.5   Clues, Guesses, Notes Chart Sample

FEEDBACK, ASSESSMENT, AND PRACTICE

Understanding the "main idea" helps people "get to the point" in verbal and written communication. Determining the main idea involves identifying the relevant clues, combining the clues with prior knowledge, and using critical thinking to guess how they fit together to create the main idea.

In addition to the communication skills developed by playing this game, the game play also requires each participant to practice impulse control. When players see the item or animal pictured on other players' cards, they must resist saying the name of that item or animal so as not to reveal the answer for another player.

For assessment purposes, the teacher can collect data on student performance of matching clues to guesses, as well as +/– observations of impulse control (resisting looking at own card, resisting blurting out what is pictured on others' cards). Continue practice by playing the game again. Once the students have experienced the game play and associated feedback, they can be prompted to provide the "teacher" feedback listed above to themselves or each other.

TEACHING FOR GENERALIZATION

One important way to teach for generalization with this game is to analyze a reading passage and identify the clues that fit together to make up the main idea. Place a reading passage, such as a paragraph, on a visual display, then model finding relevant clues. Use think-aloud strategies to model the critical thinking that leads to the main idea. Highlight relevant clues to draw attention to them and cross out irrelevant information.

Lesson 5: Relationship Types Card Sort

RELATIONSHIP TYPES CARD SORT

This card sort activity provides practice in identifying and understanding different types of relationships to help students determine the relationship types they are experiencing in the moment.

OBJECTIVES

Students will learn that there are categories of relationships and that each category contains its own set of rules governing social interactions within that relationship type. They will also learn that the category a relationship falls into can change depending upon the situation.

WHAT DOES THE RESEARCH SAY?

The content and style of our communication changes depending on the relational models we share with the people around us in any given situation. The categories used in this activity are based on Alan Fiske's original theories on relational models (Fiske, 1992).

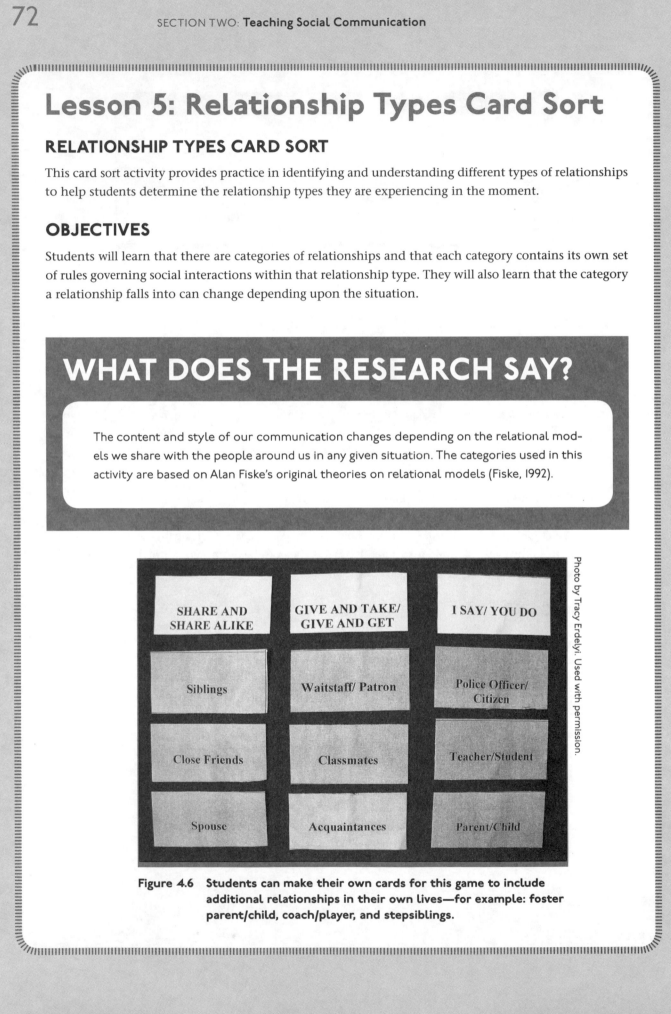

Photo by Tracy Erdelyi. Used with permission.

Figure 4.6   Students can make their own cards for this game to include additional relationships in their own lives—for example: foster parent/child, coach/player, and stepsiblings.

MATERIALS

- Relationship Types Cards (Figure 4.7 in Resources, pp. 131–132)

- Markers/chalk

- Board (whiteboard or bulletin board)

Note: *When using this activity with older students, use the relationship-type "category cards" for "Authority," "Communality," and "Reciprocity" to provide an age-appropriate level of vocabulary. When working with younger students, build understanding of relationship types by using the corresponding category cards with simpler language.*

DIRECTIONS (FOR USE WITH INDIVIDUAL STUDENTS, SMALL GROUPS, OR WHOLE CLASS)

1. Arrange the three relationship-type category cards in a row while verbally offering a definition of each. Invite students to restate each definition. Copy each definition on the board to provide a visual reference. (For larger groups, display the category cards on a whiteboard.)

2. Ask students to sort the example cards into the categories where they think each example belongs. One easy way to do this is to pull one example at a time and ask the group to decide in which category it belongs. Another approach is to have each student or pair of students draw an example card and decide where it belongs. Once the category is identified, the card is placed below, as a "column" under each category heading.

3. While students are sorting the examples, provide support to ensure that each example is sorted into the category where it most typically occurs.

4. Once the cards have been sorted, use the visual display as a reference to help students generate examples of interactions between people within each type. For example, ask the following:

   - What might your parent say to you that indicates an authority relationship?

   - When your parent says that, what should you do?

   - What might a police officer say to you?

   - How should you respond to that?

5. After identifying examples in each category, pose the question, "Do you think there is ever a time when one of these examples may fall into a different category? For example, when might a parent/child relationship *not* fall into the authority category? Students may suggest that when parents and children are playing a game together, watching a movie, or sharing a common family experience, that the relationship type could shift into the communality category. In this case, students could then shift the parent/child card out of the authority column, and into the communality column.

TALK ABOUT IT

Explore more ways that communication changes in different relationship types. Ask students for ideas about nonverbal language that changes depending on relationship type. For example, kids talking and playing on the playground (communality) might smile, laugh, and act silly. That same behavior could be considered rude if a child was doing it when a teacher asks the child to complete a task (authority).

(Continued)

(Continued)

FEEDBACK, ASSESSMENT, AND PRACTICE

Following the initial card sort activity, provide prompting throughout the school environment for students to identify relationship types and the expected communication that may be associated with those relationship types. Use supportive feedback to help students determine the correct answer, and praise when that answer has been determined. For assessment, observe students demonstrating the expected communication within a relationship type in "real time" daily social interactions.

When students have grasped the concept of relationship types, they can begin to explore the following:

- The rules for communication within each communication type and examples of how to communicate within those rules. Role-playing brief interactions can be helpful for this.

- The situational clues that indicate a relationship has just shifted from one type to another. Create a similar card sort activity to illustrate when relationship types change.

TEACHING FOR GENERALIZATION

Students can learn to generalize these concepts by identifying different relationship types within the school and in moment to moment interactions with teachers, students, and school personnel. Once students are accurately identifying relationship types within the school setting, the teacher can ask parents to have the students practice identifying relationship types at home and in the community.

Lesson 6: 5-Second Rule

5-SECOND RULE

Can you name three summer Olympic sports in five seconds? This game helps students build language and categorizing skills, with five-second turns that keep things moving.

OBJECTIVES

Students will work collaboratively to verbally generate answers that fit within a given category.

WHAT DOES THE RESEARCH SAY?

Categorizing impacts memory and a child's ability to monitor his memory. Games that include practice with categorizing are beneficial to developing memory skills (Karably & Zabrucky, 2017).

MATERIALS

- 5-Second Rule: Just Spit It Out game (PlayMonster)

DIRECTIONS (TWO PLAYERS, SMALL GROUP, OR WHOLE CLASS)

Note: *For the purposes of this lesson, the following modifications to the directions provided with the game are recommended. There are also plenty of options for customizing this game, including for age/ability levels. The recommended ages on this game are 10 through adult, but it can be adapted for younger ages, for example, by providing assistance reading the cards, extending the allowable time to answer, and reducing the number of required answers from three to two.*

1. Have students form teams. Two-person teams are ideal to start.

2. Appoint someone to be in charge of the timer.

3. The starting team draws a card from the box, which prompts them to "Name 3" of something, for example, "Name 3 types of doughnuts."

4. The team has five seconds (timer included in game) to name three of the designated item (people, animals, things).

(Continued)

(Continued)

5. If the team succeeds in naming three items before time is up, they keep the card as a means of keeping score.

6. If the team does not name three items within five seconds, they pass the card to the next team. The receiving team then tries to name the same three items within five seconds, but they may not use any of the answers given by the previous team.

7. Play continues until a team successfully names three items. That team then keeps the card.

8. The teacher or full group can decide how many points (cards collected) win the game.

TALK ABOUT IT

This game provides an opportunity to model flexible thinking. For example, if a student answers, "bagel, Boston cream, and sprinkled" as three types of doughnuts, say, "A bagel isn't usually considered a doughnut because it is less sweet and is more like bread. However, bagels are round and have a hole in the center like doughnuts and are sometimes sold alongside doughnuts, so I will be flexible and accept the answer."

FEEDBACK, ASSESSMENT, AND PRACTICE

This game provides an opportunity to observe and assess a student's ability to categorize and give answers quickly—a skill useful across all academic content within a classroom—and also to note each student's ability to collaborate effectively with a partner. It may be helpful to provide feedback on the way students collaborate to answer the game card prompt. For example, in a situation where one student on a team is giving all the answers and another student does not have a chance, consider requiring at least one answer from each member of a team. This is a fast-paced game, and students can play frequently to gain additional practice.

To practice similar collaborative communication and categorization skills with other games, try Word on the Street (p. 81) and Hedbanz (p. 69).

TEACHING FOR GENERALIZATION

Use the format of the game as a motivating approach to expand vocabulary in other situations, such as with writing assignments. For example, if a student writes, "I pulled on my boots," refer to the game and ask, "Can you name three kinds of boots?" Talk with the student about whether the more specific language makes the writing more interesting.

Lesson 7: Hidden Objects

HIDDEN OBJECTS

Highly motivating "hidden object" games engage students in thinking about what different words mean and how misinterpreting someone's words can cause a breakdown in communication.

OBJECTIVES

Students will increase their understanding of multiple meaning words. Students will increase their flexibility in understanding that words can have more than one meaning. Students will use patience for turn-taking and give supportive comments to others.

WHAT DOES THE RESEARCH SAY?

Increasing cognitive flexibility and vocabulary helps to develop problem-solving and critical thinking skills. Research supports the importance of critical thinking skill development in early childhood through high school years (Aizikovitsh-Udi, & Cheng, 2015).

MATERIALS

- Electronic tablet with Internet capability
- Any hidden object game app (purchased)

Note: *Look for games that include hidden object components that require players to interpret words in order to locate corresponding objects. Big Fish is one publisher with many diverse options, such as Hidden Expedition: Titanic. Previewing games is recommended to get a sense of the problems students will encounter before they play.*

DIRECTIONS (INDIVIDUAL STUDENTS OR SMALL GROUPS)

Note: *Using this activity with small groups adds an element of self-regulation because each student in the group takes a turn tapping the screen one time. They must inhibit the desire to tap the screen multiple times in pursuit of an object and wait for each of the other students to take turns before they tap again. The directions here are for small groups but easily adapted for use with individuals.*

(Continued)

(Continued)

1. Explain: "We are going to play a one-tap game. That means that we are going to all play this hidden object game together, and each person can tap the screen one time during his or her turn."

2. Introduce the game—for example, by saying: "This is an adventure game. You will be leading a character through solving a mystery, and along the way, there will be puzzle-solving opportunities and hidden objects to find."

3. Open the app and read the introduction to the story that the app will follow. Students can then take turns tapping one at a time on the screen to solve the puzzles and find hidden objects. Coach students as needed to each tap the screen only once and encourage those who are waiting for their turn to attend to the screen and offer help and supportive comments.

TALK ABOUT IT

This game requires critical thinking and problem-solving skills. One important aspect of problem-solving is cognitive flexibility. When students are required to find a hidden object that is identified on the list as "stamp," for example, they don't know if they are looking for a postage stamp, a date stamp, and so on. Talk with students to notice how often they find items that are either a completely different item than what they had in mind or that look different than they expected. Each time they find items that differ from their expectations, they are expanding their cognitive flexibility.

FEEDBACK, ASSESSMENT, AND PRACTICE

Provide feedback throughout the game in the form of helpful hints for solving problems and praise for problem-solving and finding hidden objects. There are usually "hint" features to these games that promote problem-solving and prevent frustration. Guide students as to when and how frequently to request hints.

There is a naturalistic assessment built into this game, since the game only progresses as problems are solved and hidden objects are found. Many of the games offer "progress" reports along the way (total numbers of objects/number of objects found). Again, many variations of these games are available, with different themes, creating opportunities for repeated practice with the target skills.

TEACHING FOR GENERALIZATION

Teachers can remind students of the problem-solving skills (such as cognitive flexibility, thinking about the problem a different way) they use during the game to solve problems in academic tasks (math for example). Teachers should coach students to remember the multiple meanings of words they have learned and ask students to apply that understanding to reading, writing, math, and science vocabulary.

Lesson 8: Ball Toss Communication

BALL TOSS COMMUNICATION

Teachers can use this active game with the entire class to build essential communication skills. In the process, students also increase their visual attention.

OBJECTIVES

Students will learn the elements of small group conversation, including gaze shifting, attention, interpreting nonverbal signals of interest, and giving and receiving information. Students will improve turn-taking in conversation and reduce interrupting and verbal outbursts.

WHAT DOES THE RESEARCH SAY?

The nonverbal communication in this activity includes shifting eye gaze toward a partner, waiting for the partner's attention, recognizing the partner is giving attention, and then taking action. These are all required elements of effective conversation (Eaves & Leathers, 2017).

MATERIALS

- One 4- to 6-inch ball (any soft play ball is fine)
- Whiteboard with markers (or blackboard with chalk)

DIRECTIONS (FOR USE WITH SMALL GROUPS)

1. Introduce the game and review directions: "We are going to play a silent ball toss game. Each person will have a chance to catch the ball." Explain that when students catch the ball, they should follow these steps:

   a. Look at one other person in the group.

   b. WAIT for that person to face you and look at you.

   c. Toss the ball to that person.

2. As a visual reminder, write and illustrate the steps (a, b, and c) on the board.

(Continued)

(Continued)

3. The teacher tosses the ball to a student to start the game. If necessary, the teacher could ask one student to help demonstrate the process before starting the game with the full group.

4. Once the silent ball toss has been completed by the full group, the teacher gives the next instruction: "Now we are going to change the game slightly. When you catch the ball, make a comment or ask a question before you complete the steps a, b, and c."

5. Game play resumes, with each student having a turn to catch the ball, speak, and toss the ball.

TALK ABOUT IT

This game highlights the reciprocity needed for good communication. Ask students what other people may be thinking when they are blurting out comments or interrupting each other. Have them discuss times they might not have been using the skill of waiting to see if a communicative partner was attending to them. Ask if the communication felt satisfying and successful or if there are ways it might have worked better.

FEEDBACK, ASSESSMENT, AND PRACTICE

It is helpful for the teacher to use the vocabulary "giving" and "receiving" when referring to the ball toss and to conversational turns. This helps to highlight the reciprocity required in communication and is more concrete for students to understand than the word "listening." Many students consider listening to be equivalent to "hearing" when, in reality, we want them to understand that listening actually means hearing plus thinking and interpreting (receiving information).

TEACHING FOR GENERALIZATION

After using this activity with students, guide them in applying the basic concepts in conversations. Refer to the game as a reminder about watching and waiting for attention during the conversation and both giving and receiving information (like tossing and catching the ball). It is especially helpful for the teacher to ask a student who has just blurted out or interrupted another, "If we were playing silent ball toss right now, which step do you think you may have missed?"

Lesson 9: Word on the Street

WORD ON THE STREET

A twist on the original directions for this game has players working in teams. They need to come to agreement quickly on their turn in order to move letter tiles over to their side.

WHAT DOES THE RESEARCH SAY?

To succeed in this game, students must use cooperation, which can translate to effective learning in the classroom. Students who participate in cooperative learning environments show positive attitudes toward the academic content, better self-esteem, and better academic achievement (Tran, 2014).

OBJECTIVES

Students will successfully collaborate to generate answers in less than a minute.

MATERIALS

- Word on the Street game (Educational Insights)

Note: *This game involves coming up with answers that match "Category Cards." Choosing those answers strategically helps players "capture" letter tiles to move them closer to their side of the game board. Only more commonly used consonants are included in the tiles, to eliminate some of the challenges with spelling associated with vowel sounds and to eliminate the difficulty of generating answers that start with less commonly used consonants, such as J or Z.*

DIRECTIONS (FOR PARTNERS OR TEAMS)

Use the directions included in the game, with the following changes:

1. Have students play in teams of two or more.

2. As long as players on a team have stated their answer and started moving the first tile prior to the timer running out, they may continue moving the remaining tiles for their answer after the timer has finished.

3. Players on a team must reach agreement for their answer prior to moving the first tile.

(Continued)

(Continued)

TALK ABOUT IT

As with 5-Second Rule (see pp. 75–76), this game requires collaboration. While 5-Second Rule requires collaboration between just two people, this game requires collaboration within a larger group, as the teams in this game could be up to ten people. Assign group sizes based on the desired amount of collaborative input from each group member. Larger teams may allow for some players to avoid participating, so observe and modify group sizes as needed.

In addition to the communication skills used in this game (collaboration and categorizing), there are added strategic elements that are helpful skills for self-regulation. Players are practicing the self-regulatory skills of flexibility, forethought, and self-reflection. For example, in order to move the most letter tiles over to their side, players must choose answers that

- Have a greater number of consonants
- Strategically move tiles toward their side or prevent the opponent from moving tiles off the board ("capturing" them)
- Include consonants that are not already acquired by the other team

Therefore, they must use flexibility to change an answer as a team as needed for the best outcome. Players use forethought to plan which of their answers will get them the most tiles and self-reflection when they realize after their turn how a different answer may have gained them even more tiles.

FEEDBACK, ASSESSMENT, AND PRACTICE

Provide students with feedback about checking in with teammates to ensure everyone has reached agreement on an answer prior to anyone on the team moving the first tile. As needed, provide feedback as to whether an answer fits the assigned category or not. For assessment purposes, this game provides opportunities to collect data on each student's collaborative skills such as with

- Offering ideas
- Considering others' ideas
- Changing an answer to agree with group
- Offering compliments and supportive comments to other group members

TEACHING FOR GENERALIZATION

Identify other opportunities for students to use collaboration skills, such as during small group work or activities. To add a game-like element, using the timer in Word on the Street, challenge groups to generate an agreed upon idea in less than a minute.

Lesson 10: Beanbag Crash

BEANBAG CRASH

This activity incorporates negotiation, cooperation, and collaboration in a fun, active way.

OBJECTIVES

Students will learn to combine their own ideas with a partner's idea to carry out a collaborative plan.

WHAT DOES THE RESEARCH SAY?

In this activity, communication for forming a collaborative plan is broken down into simple, concrete steps (the script for "mixing ideas"). In the process, students learn how to share ideas to come up with and carry out a collaborative plan. Gehlbach et al. (2015) show that "developing the capacity to take the perspective of others is an especially promising approach to promoting more effective conflict resolution" (p. 531).

MATERIALS

- Five to six beanbag "chairs"
- Mixing Ideas Mission Visual (Figure 4.8, p. 133) or a small whiteboard to display the script

DIRECTIONS (FOR PARTNERS)

1. Have students place the beanbags in a pile.

2. Introduce the activity: "You are going to work with your partner to decide how to safely crash into that pile of beanbags at the same time. To come up with a plan, you're going to use the steps for mixing ideas. Your goal is to mix your ideas together and to crash into the beanbag pile together."

3. Share the steps/script for mixing ideas:

   Student 1: My idea is _____. What do you think?

   Student 1: (Wait and receive information.)

(Continued)

(Continued)

Student 2: I think_____. I would like to _____. What do you think?

Student 2: (Wait and receive information.)

Repeat these steps as needed.

4. Have students use the script to share their ideas and make a plan. An example might look like this:

Student 1: My idea is to hop to the beanbags and crash into them. What do you think?

Student 2: I think it is a good idea. I would like to run and crash into the beanbags. What do you think?

Student 1: How about we hop four times and then run the rest of the way to the beanbags? What do you think?

Student 2: Okay, let's do it!

5. Have students move 10 to 15 feet away from the beanbag pile, then carry out their plan. Once they have crashed into the beanbags, ask them to evaluate their plan: How did it work out? Did you crash into the beanbag at the same time? Offer feedback and praise for carrying out the steps to mix their ideas together.

TIP

Beanbag Crash involves physical activity such as running, jumping, skipping, spinning, and "crashing," and should ideally take place outdoors or in a large, obstacle-free environment, under close supervision. There are many alternatives for a less physically involved opportunity to "mix ideas." For example, modify a game of Suspend (pp. 24–26) to include the script for mixing ideas. (See Directions, Step 4.) Working collaboratively to get all the rods hanging on the structure, students can "mix" their ideas before deciding where to place the rods. Other cooperative building activities, such as those with Lego or K'nex structures, also work well to teach negotiation, cooperation, and collaboration.

TALK ABOUT IT

This activity breaks down the communication used for cooperation and honoring another's ideas. Talk with students about the ideas they liked best. Also have them reflect on the process: "How did sharing ideas increase or decrease the fun?" and "Were there any times you heard someone else's idea but then forgot to include it?"

FEEDBACK, ASSESSMENT, AND PRACTICE

Teachers can

- Ask students to give feedback about what worked, what did not work, and how they felt about the experience

- Use observation to assess whether students are using the script, mixing ideas, and carrying out the plan they made

- Have students practice the steps for mixing ideas by taking several turns during the activity and by pairing with different students throughout the activity.

TEACHING FOR GENERALIZATION

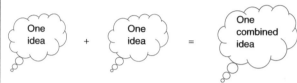

Mixing Ideas Mission

Use the steps for mixing ideas in your everyday life at home and at school. The steps are the following:

1. SAY your idea or plan. Examples:
    - My idea is _____.
    - I want to _____.
    - How about if we _____?

2. ASK the other person (or people), "What do you think?" Then LISTEN and THINK about the other person's answer.

3. MIX the two ideas together.

One idea + One idea = One combined idea

When you get caught by your teacher or parent mixing ideas together, you get two things:

1. Mixing idea <u>points</u> to bring back to group

2. A <u>reputation</u> with your friends and family that you are considerate, flexible, and easy to work with

Figure 4.8   Mixing Ideas Mission Visual

Use the script for mixing ideas when students are working to create small group projects or complete assignments together. Students can use the script to practice cooperation in other situations as well, such as with coming up with a plan to do something with a friend or family member. (See Figure 4.8, Mixing Ideas Mission Visual, above.)

Teaching Perspective-Taking

CHAPTER FIVE

Perspective-Taking
The Basics

The world as we have created it is a process of our thinking.
It cannot be changed without changing our thinking.

—Albert Einstein

Joe: Where are we planning to go?

John: We are heading to the parking garage.

Joe: When I ask you, "Where are we planning to go?" I want you to say, "Moe's."

I overheard this conversation between a son and his father while waiting for an elevator. I instantly recognized Joe's body language as slightly aloof—somewhat distant in both space and content from his communicative partner. When I heard him correct John for not recognizing the desired scripted response, I realized that the conversation was about more than just one young man preferring to go to Moe's. Joe may indeed like to go to Moe's, but most likely, more than going to a preferred place, Joe likes getting a predictable response when he initiates conversations. If the response is predictable (he knows what the partner is going to say), he can feel an increased sense of safety and confidence whenever he initiates conversation in that way. John did not immediately understand Joe's intention when he heard the question, so he answered based on their shared location and gave the information he thought Joe was seeking. Their interaction highlights the importance of perspective-taking, or understanding each other's intentions when we are conversing.

This chapter will examine some historical research related to perspective-taking, some informal tasks for assessing *theory of mind* (ToM) impairments and some content areas for teaching perspective-taking to students.

THEORY OF MIND

Perspective-taking refers to the ability to infer the thoughts, feelings, and beliefs of others and then consider how they relate to one's own thoughts, feelings, and beliefs. To navigate the social world, individuals must also consider how their communicative behavior affects their communicative partner. The term theory of mind is sometimes used synonymously with perspective-taking. Theory of mind is the ability to recognize and attribute mental states—thoughts, perceptions, desires, intentions, feelings—to oneself and to others and to understand how these mental states might affect behavior. Theory of mind is also an understanding that others have beliefs, thought processes, and emotions completely separate from our own (Pedersen, 2018).

Theory of mind development has significant implications on a child's or adult's daily social interactions (Repacholi & Slaughter, 2004). When a student doesn't have the understanding that others have completely separate thought processes and emotions, misunderstandings like the following might occur:

> **Teacher:**   Why didn't you come in from recess with the rest of your class?
>
> **Student:**   You <u>know</u> I didn't hear the bell!

The teacher wasn't outside at recess and had no way of knowing that the student did not hear the bell. The student believes (due to impaired theory of mind) that the teacher already knows everything he knows and therefore already knows he did not hear the bell. How exasperating it must be for people with theory of mind deficits to explain their thinking to others, when they believe they are repeating information that is already known to everyone.

Theory of mind and perspective-taking are terms that encompass so many broad concepts (thoughts, perceptions, beliefs, desires, and feelings) that trying to define each specific aspect results in its own manuscript. For explicit definitions and a developmental scope and sequence of theory of mind, please reference *Theory of Mind Atlas* (Hutchins & Prelock, 2016). *Theory of Mind Atlas* is a valuable resource for understanding the complexities of perspective-taking.

SOCIAL COGNITIVE THEORY

Albert Bandura (1989) described *vicarious learning capability* as one of the necessary components of social cognitive development. This capability is the ability to learn through the experiences of others. In order to learn through the experiences of others, children must understand the impact (thoughts and feelings) of an experience on another person.

For example, students who are able to do vicarious learning hear the teacher remind a classmate to use a quiet voice and realize that it is a good idea for them to quiet down as well. Children with impaired vicarious learning see the teacher tell a classmate to quiet down and go on talking loudly, thinking there is no need for them to modify their own actions.

INFORMAL ASSESSMENT TASKS

There are many ways to informally assess perspective-taking skills. The three types of assessments that follow assess different aspects of perspective-taking:

- Emotional knowledge

- Theory of mind development through understanding of the false beliefs of another person

- Typically understood social conventions through identification of faux pas scenarios

HEIDER AND SIMMEL VIDEO

How do we overlay our emotional knowledge onto geometric shapes that have no facial expressions, no voice tone, and no body language?

Psychologists Fritz Heider and Marianne Simmel (1944) created a short (two minute), now classic video of two-dimensional geometric shapes, in silent, black and white animation. The shapes, moving around on the screen, "interact" with each other—or so it seems as interpreted by people who overlay their emotional knowledge onto the shapes. The shapes have no facial expressions, no bodies to show body language, and they don't talk. This video is readily available online. (Search Heider and Simmel video.)

How is it that when people watch this video, they are able to tell a story using human attributes such as bullying, fear, anger, friendship, and happiness? Asking a person who has never seen this video to watch it and then tell the story of what it showed is a good way to gain insight into that person's emotional knowledge and ability to interpret thoughts, feelings, and human attributes. When these perspective-taking skills are solid, the person tells the story and lists attributes such as those described above. When these skills are impaired, the person gives a very explicit description of the shapes and their movement on the screen.

FALSE BELIEF TASKS

False belief tasks examine a child's ability to understand that others either do or do not share that child's knowledge. Developmentally, a child typically demonstrates the ability to infer the understanding of another's knowledge (tested through verbally presented tasks, which follow) by the age of four years.

Sally–Anne Task

An experiment that became known as the "Sally–Anne task" is one example of a false-belief task. The Sally–Anne task, developed by Wimmer and Perner (1983), uses sketches to examine children's understanding of another person's incorrect (or "false") belief. The sample that follows is a basic version of this task.

SALLY–ANNE TASK

1. Sally is playing with her doll. When she is finished, she puts the doll away in the toy box and leaves the room.

2. Anne comes into the room, finds the doll in the toy box, and plays with it. When she is finished, she puts the doll away in the dresser and leaves the room.

3. Sally returns to the room.

4. Where will Sally look for the doll?

The child with typically well-developed theory of mind will answer, "Sally will look in the toy box," and if asked why, the child will reply, "Because Sally doesn't know the doll was moved." The child with delayed or impaired theory of mind development will answer, "Sally will look in the dresser," and if asked why, will state, "Because that is where the doll is."

Marbles Task

In this task, the child is shown a box of coloring crayons. The examiner asks what the child thinks is in the box, and the child likely answers, "crayons." The examiner then removes the crayons from the box, showing the child the crayons have been removed.

The examiner then shows the child a handful of marbles and asks the child to watch as he puts the marbles into the crayon box and closes the lid. The examiner asks the child what is now in the box, and the child likely answers, "marbles." The examiner asks the child, "If we take this box into the next room where your mom is waiting and we ask your mom what is in the box, what do you think your mom will say?" The child with typically well-developed theory of mind will answer "crayons," and if asked why, will state, "Because Mom did not see the crayons taken out and the marbles put in."

FAUX PAS TEST

Understanding whether or not a person has committed a social faux pas depends on solid perspective-taking capabilities. Developmentally, this skill is acquired by ages nine through eleven years. Baron-Cohen, O'Riordan, Jones, Stone, and Plaisted (1999) developed a series of "faux pas" stories for children, which were later adapted for adults. In both versions, one of the characters in the story either does or does not commit a faux pas. A faux pas was defined as a situation where "a speaker says something without considering if it is something that the listener might not want to hear or know, and which typically has negative consequences that the speaker never intended" (Baron-Cohen et al., 1999, p. 408). The child (or adult) reads the story, then determines whether or not a character in the story committed a faux pas.

Some research (Thiébaut et al., 2015) suggests that the adult with impaired perspective-taking ability might *over* identify the faux pas, identifying that a person has committed a faux pas when he has not. A nice feature of these stories is that they describe several different types of social situations. Incorrect responses to the questions about a particular story could indicate which social situations a person finds harder to interpret.

THE INTERSECTION OF PERSPECTIVE-TAKING AND SOCIAL COMMUNICATION

Once perspective-taking capabilities have been assessed and any deficits have been identified, addressing those deficits though instruction becomes critically important. In order to teach perspective-taking skills, it is necessary to understand the intersection of perspective-taking and social communication. The intersection of perspective-taking and social communication can best be described using examples of the impacts of individual knowledge versus mutual knowledge:

- Maheen knows she is having a surprise party for Eva.

- Roberto knows that Maheen is having a surprise party for Eva.

- Maheen knows that Roberto knows that Maheen is having a surprise party for Eva.

- Roberto knows that Maheen knows that Roberto knows that Maheen is having a surprise party for Eva.

The first two statements, "Maheen knows that . . ." and "Roberto knows that . . ." Are examples of *individual knowledge.* The remaining statements are descriptions of *mutual knowledge* (Pinker, 2008). The challenge with individual knowledge versus mutual knowledge is that each type of knowledge sets up an expectation as to what people are supposed to say or do.

- Do either Maheen or Roberto think that Eva knows that Maheen is having a surprise party for Eva?

- Does Eva know that Maheen is having a surprise party for her?

In the first statement, when only Maheen knows that she is having a surprise party for Eva, Maheen knows that she won't say anything to Eva about the party to avoid ruining the surprise. Maheen also will not tell anyone that she thinks will tell Eva, so that Eva does not find out about the party ahead of time. When Maheen invites Roberto to the party, she will mention that the party is a surprise, so that Roberto will realize he should not talk to Eva about the party. When Roberto knows that Maheen knows about the party, they have a mutual expectation that neither will ruin the surprise by talking either to Eva or to others who may talk to Eva about the party. In this way, our knowledge of our own thoughts and others' thoughts creates the rules for our communication and our actions. Let's take this example into a classroom situation:

- The teacher knows the rule during silent reading is "no talking."

- The student knows the rule during silent reading is "no talking."

- The teacher knows the student knows the rule during reading is "no talking."

- The student knows the teacher knows the student knows the rule during reading is "no talking."

If the understanding of individual knowledge is solid, only one person knows not to talk. If the understanding of mutual knowledge is solid, both people know that neither should talk. What happens if a portion of that knowledge is interpreted differently, such as in the following examples?

- A student interprets "the rule during silent reading is 'no talking'" as meaning, "When I am silently reading I should not talk, but if I am not reading at the moment, talking is okay."

- The teacher interprets the rule as "Throughout the entire period of time designated for silent reading, no one should be talking."

In the scenario described above, there is individual knowledge but not mutual knowledge, which means that the student is likely to say or do things that the teacher is not expecting, such as talking during silent reading. These "rules" that govern our social behavior that are dictated by our perspective-taking can be referred to as the "hidden curriculum."

HIDDEN CURRICULUM

In *The Hidden Curriculum: Practical Solutions for Understanding Unstated Rules in Social Situations* (2004), Myles, Trautman, and Schelvan write about social customs and rules that are not explicitly taught, but rather society assumes people automatically know them.

The Hidden Curriculum addresses many everyday social challenges. One example is the common classroom scenario of students who constantly raise their hands to say, "Call on me!" indicating a failure to recognize that others may find this behavior annoying. This book is an excellent resource for teachers, parents, and others working with children who have social-cognitive learning challenges, and it can be a helpful tool for teaching children how to navigate confusing social situations. Even more importantly, it raises awareness that there are endless hidden rules that can be confusing to children and adults need to continually assess the social rules that they assume children already know. A few such rules that have been brought to my attention recently include the following:

- How does a student know which adults are safe to talk to and which are strangers?

- How does a student know when a joke is funny to others?

- How does a student know when touching other students (pushing, hair pulling, bumping into) is rude/bullying/harassing, versus when it is playful horseplay?

- How does a student know when insults and put-downs are being used as friendly, competitive banter versus when they are being used to be hurtful?

The answers to these questions are very complex because none of them have just one answer. Some of the answers relate back to understanding the relationship types described in the chapter in this book on Social Communication (see pp. 53–60), but other answers rely on the student's social knowledge of others' beliefs, feelings, intentions, and thoughts. That understanding then guides which things the student should say or do within a specific interaction. Consider the common scenario of one student doing something to a classmate that is unintentionally irritating, rude, or even invasive. Here's a familiar example:

Leo is pulling on his friend Jenny's ponytail and laughing.

Jenny tells him to stop, telling him, "I don't like when you pull my hair."

Leo says, "But it is funny," and pulls her hair again.

In this case, Leo needed to remember that experiences he finds funny are not necessarily found funny by others sharing the experience—that people can have different thoughts and feelings about the same experience. But Leo also needs to figure out a much more complicated puzzle: Why can he see other teenagers do that same action to their friends, and in those situations, it is considered friendly horseplay or even a show of affection, and in his situation it is considered annoying?

Leo is trying to imitate the actions he sees his peers doing, but he is missing the nuanced hidden rule that he needs to predict the other person's thoughts and feelings, in this case Jenny's, about the interaction before he does it. He also needs to have the larger social context of the physical interaction, which kinds of interactions are social "trends" among teens, and which are not.

For students with social-cognitive challenges like Leo and students in general, understanding the hidden curriculum surrounding teen interactions can help prevent social misunderstandings, such as annoying others when they are trying to be playful. It can be helpful to teach students a "rule" they can use in situations where the expected behavior is unclear to them—for example, "If the other person and I have both enjoyed this interaction previously, it is okay to do it. If I do not have this shared history with a person, it is not okay to perform that interaction."

LEVELS OF FRIENDSHIP

Understanding the hidden curriculum *of relationships* is challenging to those with impaired perspective-taking. Jeanette McAfee, MD, in *Navigating the Social World: A Curriculum for Individuals With Asperger's Syndrome, High Functioning Autism and Related Disorders* (2013), uses a diagram of concentric circles as a helpful visual to explore levels of "closeness" in relationship. (See Figure 5.1, p. 96.)

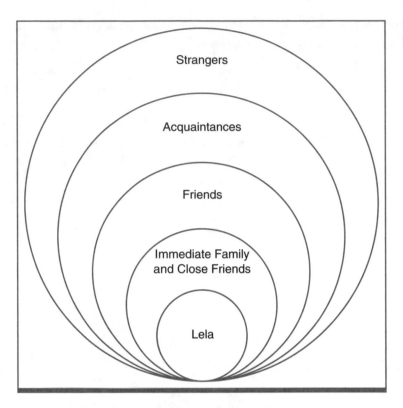

Figure 5.1   Levels of Friendship. Jeanette McAfee, MD (2013), calls this concentric circle visual a "Privacy Circles Chart."

To use this approach with students, start by drawing four to six concentric circles on a sheet of paper. For purposes of this example, let's make this a student named Lela. Beginning with the center circle, place Lela's name or picture in the center circle. Ask Lela, "Who are the people that should go in the next circle?" Help Lela understand that the people who go in the circle closest to her name (or picture) are the people she feels closest to. This includes people that Lela can walk up to and hug or touch, share affectionate language with, or even interrupt at times, and all of the people will feel comfortable with these words and actions. Lela might decide that her mom, dad, brother, and dog belong in that circle. Perhaps Lela might include good friends, cousins, or grandparents as well.

In the next circle, Lela considers, "Who are some people I see regularly but who are not as close as my family and close friends?" This circle might show classmates, regular acquaintances, teachers, or distant relatives. These people give friendly greetings to each other, maintain memory of each other's life events, and share a reserved level of personal information with one another.

The next circle would contain the names or pictures of even more distant relationships for Lela. These could include infrequent people she sees (acquaintances) or occasionally service providers, such as a mail carrier or cashier. These people give friendly greetings and might discuss the weather but do not share personal information about themselves. Lela likely does not know their names and can follow the social "rule" of not sharing too much information about herself with them.

SYSTEMATIC TEACHING FOR INDIVIDUAL VERSUS MUTUAL KNOWLEDGE

The board games Clue and Suspicion require players to use their knowledge of other players' knowledge to successfully navigate the game. In Suspicion, players must ask if a different player's "character" can "see" a target character. In the game, "see" is defined as being in a straight horizontal or vertical line with the character but not in a diagonal line. In asking the question, the player gains information that helps him to deduce which characters the other player can or cannot be. See the lesson plan for playing Suspicion on page 109.

LISTEN, CARE, CHANGE

"Listening" is a means of receiving information. Traditionally, we think of people listening with their ears. However, when we listen to people, we are receiving information through our ears and eyes and even our physical proximity. The act of listening in this way is a critical part of social communication, but it is useless without the brain then processing the information to apply social meaning.

The interpretation of that information is perspective-taking. The Listen, Care, Change strategy shows the connection between peoples' thoughts and feelings and their words and actions, demonstrating for the learner that thoughts and feelings lead to words and actions and that the words and actions we use impact the thoughts and feelings of others, which will thereby impact their words and actions. Listen, Care, Change empowers the learner to understand that we can influence the way others think about us. We can change our actions in a way that makes others feel good about us and that makes us feel good about ourselves.

See pp. 115–117 for a lesson plan on teaching the Listen, Care, Change strategy.

COMIC STRIP CONVERSATIONS AND SOCIAL STORIES

"Comic strip conversations" and "social stories" are strategies for teaching social understanding to people with autism. Created by Carol Gray, these strategies are so effective they have become indispensable tools for use with anyone who is struggling to understand social situations or concepts.

What people think and feel is as important as what they say and do. Comic strip conversations (Gray, 1994) are a way to represent this, showing both the words and actions a person is using as well as that person's thoughts and feelings. When using comic strip conversations with students, it is helpful to label (name or initials) each person depicted (such as with a stick figure), as well as that person's speech balloons and thought bubbles and any relevant actions. Cartoons should also contain a reference in the corner of the page that shows the location of the situation depicted. The reference of location is important because the rules that govern social interactions change in different locations. For example, it is expected social behavior to run around and yell on the playground but not expected social behavior to run around and yell in the classroom.

Social stories (Gray, 2015) are short stories designed to increase a person's social understanding of an event or situation. They are highly effective for students, but this strategy must be used with fidelity as described in Gray's book on the subject. Many people learn about social stories without explicit training from Gray or without reading her book, and this can be problematic because they create social stories that do not follow the prescribed formula then become puzzled and disappointed when the stories don't "work."

When writing social stories, important elements to remember are that the stories are written to increase social understanding and are never written to change a specific behavior. Because behaviors often change when social understanding improves, it can be very tempting to write stories to change behavior. In addition, social stories have specific sentence types, such as "directive," "perspective," "affirming," and "descriptive." The ratio of one sentence type to the others is critical to the effectiveness of the story "working" to increase social understanding and in keeping the reader enthusiastic about reading the stories.

In addition to their usefulness for assessment, the informal assessment tasks described in this chapter can also be used for teaching perspective-taking. During the administration of any of the assessment tasks discussed in this chapter, the teacher can model providing the answers that accurately interpret others' thoughts and can explain the thought process and rationale behind those answers. In addition, the strategies identified to teach perspective-taking are a few brief examples based on a wide variety of resources. By beginning with understanding the foundational importance of perspective-taking and using modeling and verbal narration to describe one's own thoughts and feelings and those of others, teachers and parents can successfully incorporate perspective-taking skill development into activities of daily living.

The chapter that follows, "Lesson Plans for Teaching Perspective-Taking," offers ten lesson plans for activities and games to teach perspective-taking skills, providing for the "in the moment" learning and practice children need to generalize skills in new situations. As you use these activities and games with students, keep the following tips in mind:

- Students may need to be given answers at first. If a student is having difficulty guessing another person's thoughts or feelings, offer some probable options.

- "Good," "bad," and "okay" are not "emotion words." When students use these words, ask them to name the emotion that accompanies the feeling.

- Stick with it. Like self-regulation and social communication skills, perspective-taking is learned with repetition and practice. While significant progress may happen quickly, time is necessary for sustained progress.

- Refer to What Does the Research Say? in each lesson to learn more about how each game or activity supports the development of perspective-taking. For example, several games and activities involve collaboration, negotiation, and empathy, which research shows aid in understanding others' thoughts and feelings.

CHAPTER SIX

Lesson Plans for Teaching Perspective-Taking

Table 6.1   Perspective-Taking Lesson Plans Overview

Game/Activity	Areas of Focus	Page
Apples to Apples Personalized	Positive thoughts about self and others	100
Celebrity	Using clues to guess identity	102
Telephone in Pictures and Words	Interpreting the meaning of others' words and drawings	104
Spoons	Quickly shift thinking between self and others	106
Suspicion	See another's "point of view"	109
Picture Sequencing Activity	Using social context to tell a story	111
Faceland	Learn to interpret six universal emotions	113
Listen, Care, Change	Words and actions impact on self and others	115
Guess My Gaze	Following eye gaze to guess others' thoughts	118
Bubble Talk	Use funny captions to think about others' thoughts	120

Lesson 1: Apples to Apples Personalized

"APPLES TO APPLES" PERSONALIZED

This game is all about being able to anticipate how the "judge" will think.

OBJECTIVES

Players will increase the flexibility of their perspective-taking skills by considering multiple and sometimes humorous descriptions of how others see them.

WHAT DOES THE RESEARCH SAY?

Playing this game requires students to think about what others are thinking and what others like and dislike, essentially using their perspective-taking skills to have the best chance of playing a winning card. The development of perspective-taking skills shows positive impact on social-interaction skills and general vocabulary ability (Bosacki & Astington, 1999).

MATERIALS

- Apples to Apples game (Mattel; either the "Junior" or original version)
- Index cards
- Pens (and/or pencils, crayons, markers)

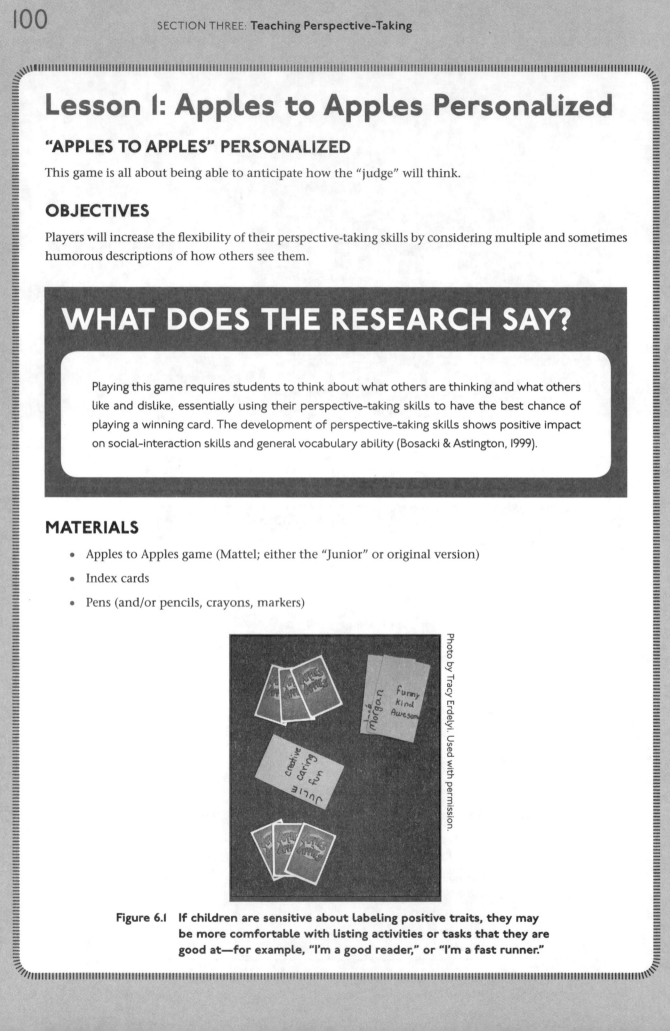

Photo by Tracy Erdelyi. Used with permission.

Figure 6.1   If children are sensitive about labeling positive traits, they may be more comfortable with listing activities or tasks that they are good at—for example, "I'm a good reader," or "I'm a fast runner."

DIRECTIONS (SMALL GROUPS WORK BEST FOR THE PURPOSES OF THIS GAME)

Note: *Apples to Apples has two different sets of cards: Red cards have the name of a person, place, thing, or event, along with a related fact or comment. Green cards have a "description" word (such as "fun" or "spotless," along with other words that have a similar meaning. For the purposes of this game, students will be creating new "green" cards to tell about themselves. Players should have some experience playing Apples to Apples before adding this personalized twist.*

1. Give students index cards to create new green cards. Have them write their name on one card, along with three positive words or phrases that describe them—for example, Tess: kind, funny, friendly. Provide green cards from the game for students to use as a model.

2. Next, have each student create a green card for each of the other players in the group. If there are four players, for example, this will result in each player creating four new green cards in all. There will now be four green cards with each player's name, for a total of 16 new cards.

3. Play the game using the newly created green cards in place of the green cards provided with the game, shuffling these cards and placing them facedown in the center.

4. The "judge" in each round turns over the green card on top, and play continues, with players selecting the best red card from their hand to go with that green card.

TALK ABOUT IT

Ask students how they use perspective-taking skills when they play this game. Do they interpret others' intended meanings or humor? In this game, the positive characteristics listed on each person's name card reveal what they think about themselves and what others think about them. Remind students that our thoughts and feelings affect our words and actions and that using positive thoughts can lead to positive actions.

FEEDBACK, ASSESSMENT, AND PRACTICE

When playing this game, students will be receiving compliments in the form of those three positive descriptors from each of the other players. Students may have difficulty accepting positive feedback, and careful attention and support should be provided. Provide verbal supports for accepting compliments, such as "You can just say, 'Thank you.'" Model appropriate use of humor when needed in response to the selected red cards.

TEACHING FOR GENERALIZATION

After playing this game, students can practice generating descriptors for other people they know, such as family members and friends, working toward generating descriptors about new people they meet. This practice provides the opportunity for them to develop early impressions about people and then analyze those impressions as they learn more about people and their relationships.

Lesson 2: Celebrity

CELEBRITY

This Charades-like team game is a fun way to engage students in looking at others' points of view.

OBJECTIVES

Students will use gestalt processing (putting details together to determine the main idea) to put together relevant social clues and knowledge about others (perspective-taking) to make accurate guesses as to the identity of a famous person that matches relevant clues.

WHAT DOES THE RESEARCH SAY?

The clue-givers in this game are thinking about the name they are trying to get others to guess. The guessers are using their perspective-taking skills to guess what the clue-givers are thinking. Understanding each other's thoughts is a valuable tool for collaborative learning in the classroom and beyond. In the workplace, research shows that perspective-taking skills lead to new and useful ideas (Grant & Berry, 2011).

MATERIALS

- Paper (cut into small strips)
- Pens or pencils
- Timer (30 seconds to 1 minute)
- Bowl or bag (to hold the strips)

DIRECTIONS (MINIMUM OF FOUR PLAYERS, UP TO TWENTY OR MORE; THE FUN INCREASES WITH MORE PEOPLE)

1. Each player takes five to ten strips of paper (decide based on the desired length of the game).

2. Players write a single "celebrity" name on each strip of paper. This can be the name of a famous actor, fictional character, historical figure, cartoon character, politician, even any of the people playing the game! (See Teaching for Generalization.)

3. Give players time to come up with names (one name per strip). Remind players to keep the names they choose private. Collect all the strips in a bowl and "stir" them up.

4. Create two teams ("A" and "B" here). Team A chooses a person to be the first clue giver. The clue giver randomly chooses a paper from the bowl, sets the timer, then begins giving clues to help Team A guess the name. Remind players as needed that they can't say the name or any part of the name as a clue.

Example:

Clue Giver: This is a famous Disney cartoon character.

Guessers: Donald Duck!

Clue Giver: He has round ears and knows someone named Minnie.

Guessers: Mickey Mouse!

5. Once a player makes a correct guess, the clue giver puts that strip aside and chooses another from the bowl. Team A continues playing until time runs out.

6. Play shifts now to Team B. Team B proceeds with the same steps as Team A, choosing a clue giver who gives clues until time is up. For each new round, Teams A and B choose a different clue giver.

7. Teams can keep a tally of correct guesses to keep score.

TALK ABOUT IT

Ask students how they used perspective-taking skills to guess the celebrity. Were they able to predict which clues their teammates would most easily recognize as being about a specific person? Discuss how successful predictions about others' knowledge leads to successful clues. Have them also notice that gestalt processing skills are used for the guessers to put the clues together to make an accurate guess.

FEEDBACK, ASSESSMENT, AND PRACTICE

Feedback is immediate and positive when team members guess the correct answer, and because there are multiple guessers, there is frequently a positive result. If players have difficulty coming up with clues, a helper from the team can jump in to make the clue-giving experience more positive and successful.

TEACHING FOR GENERALIZATION

Adapt this game to incorporate a blend of people students know in their own lives (along with the "celebrities"). Include names of some of the students playing the game and other people known to the team—for example, the music teacher and the principal. Or play it using only the names of those playing the game.

Lesson 3: Telephone in Pictures and Words

TELEPHONE IN PICTURES AND WORDS

The more players in this group storytelling game, the more fun it becomes.

OBJECTIVES

Participants will improve perspective-taking by interpreting the written communication and drawings of others. Each player must interpret the meaning of another person's words or illustration and write or draw that interpretation on paper. To accomplish this, each player must think about what the other players were thinking.

WHAT DOES THE RESEARCH SAY?

In this game, students use drawing and writing to share their ideas and collaboratively tell a story. Research shows that collaborative activities using picture books improve students' perspective-taking and self-regulation skills (An, Lee, & Kwon, 2019).

MATERIALS

- Paper (cut into approximately 4" × 5" pieces; each player needs as many pieces of paper as there are players)

- Pencils (one per player)

- Crayons, markers

Photo by Tracy Erdelyi. Used with permission.

Figure 6.2   Like the classic game of Telephone, the "story" in this game changes as players pass it on, in this case, based on other players' pictures and written words.

DIRECTIONS (FOR FIVE TO TWENTY PLAYERS; THE MORE THE MERRIER)

1. Gather players in a circle or around a table. Distribute a stack of paper and a pencil to each player.

2. All players write a single simple sentence on the top sheet of paper in their stack.

3. Each player then passes the entire stack of papers to the person to the left.

4. The receiving player silently reads the sentence on the paper.

5. The receiving player then moves the top sheet of paper (with the sentence on it) to the bottom of the stack and continues the game by drawing a picture to illustrate that sentence.

6. Once all players have completed their drawings, they again pass the entire stack of papers to the person to the left.

7. The receiving player looks at the picture, places it on the bottom of the stack, and then proceeds to write a sentence on the top sheet of paper to caption that picture.

8. Play continues by repeating this process of alternately writing a sentence and drawing a picture until the stack of paper makes its way back to the original author.

9. Each player then lays out the slips of paper from beginning to end and tells a story by reading aloud each sentence and showing the accompanying illustrations.

TALK ABOUT IT

In addition to perspective-taking, this game also uses humor, which can enhance bonding and rapport building through a shared humorous experience. Social communication is addressed as well, highlighting the importance of how verbal tone and facial expression influence the meaning of a sentence.

FEEDBACK, ASSESSMENT, AND PRACTICE

Teachers should use the sharing time for each story to have students identify what they were thinking when they read a sentence or looked at a picture and compare this to what the person who wrote that sentence or drew that picture was thinking. There is a natural opportunity for this when one player notices that another player has incorrectly interpreted a drawing.

This game can be played repeatedly, with new stories and outcomes every time.

TEACHING FOR GENERALIZATION

Students can practice sharing and understanding different perspectives by viewing a single picture as a group and generating their own captions for the picture. Once the captions have been developed, the teacher can read them aloud and students can guess which caption was written by which student. This provides the added practice of not only understanding how another person interprets a picture but also how all of the students can share the same experience (viewing the same picture) and have differing interpretations and responses.

Lesson 4: Spoons

SPOONS

In this familiar card game, the ability to keep an eye on the other players is a good idea.

OBJECTIVES

Students will increase their use of joint attention, an important underlying skill in the development of theory of mind.

WHAT DOES THE RESEARCH SAY?

When playing Spoons, students keep in mind the cards they are trying to match in their own hands, while noticing and remembering how many of a certain card have been picked up by another player, thereby using memory while thinking about themselves and others. Developing perspective-taking and memory skills yields positive results. Research shows that students' social network size is increased as their perspective-taking and memory capacity improves (Stiller & Dunbar, 2007).

MATERIALS

- Deck of cards (remove jokers and wild cards)
- Spoons (one fewer than the number of players)

DIRECTIONS (FOR TWO TO EIGHT PLAYERS; IF ADDING MORE PLAYERS, USE EXTRA SPOONS AND AN EXTRA DECK OF CARDS)

Note: *Play can be varied to include any number of rounds that time allows. If a player needs to leave the game, a spoon is simply removed from the pile in the center and the remaining players can continue. There is more than one way to play this game. This is one version.*

1. Gather players in a circle or around a table. Place the spoons (one less than the number of players) in the center. Explain that the goal of this card game is to get four of a kind. Review what happens when a player gets four of a kind:

   The first player to get four of a kind takes a spoon (four of the same number or four of the same face card). When players observe another player taking a spoon, they also take a spoon. Remind players that only the first player to take a spoon needs to have four of a kind. The last player to notice that a player has four of a kind will not get a spoon. This player loses the round and is assigned a letter, starting with S (for Spoon). Players who lose more than one round continue getting letters. Any player who spells Spoon *is eliminated from the game, and one spoon is then removed from play.*

2. To start the game, choose one player to be the dealer. This player deals four cards to each player then stacks the remaining cards nearby.

3. The dealer takes the top card from the stack and uses a "Do I want this card or not?" thought process to decide whether to keep the card. Either way, the dealer discards one card facedown to the player on the left.

4. That player picks up the card, follows the same "Do I want this card or not?" thought process, and then discards one card facedown to the player on the left.

5. Play continues, with each player picking up a card and then passing a card facedown to the next player. The last player to pick up a card discards one card to a "discard" pile.

6. The dealer then takes another card from the stack, and the process begins again. This continues until a player gets four of a kind or there are no more cards to play.

7. Should the dealer use the entire deck without anyone getting four of a kind, play continues using the discarded cards from the last player.

8. Once a player gets four of a kind, the deal can pass to the next player on the left, with all players having a chance to be the dealer if time allows.

TALK ABOUT IT

Talk with students about how variations in spoon placement can affect game play. If metal spoons are used, for example, and piled on top of each other, the first player to take a spoon is likely to make noise, providing an auditory alert to all of the other players to take a spoon. If the spoons are spaced out, where many players can easily reach, they can each take a spoon quietly and easily, perhaps avoiding the notice of others.

After playing, ask students how many different things they attended to in order to get a spoon. Did they all share the similar experience of monitoring their own hands while maintaining their attention on the shared pile of spoons in the center? Explain that this "experience sharing" process is called "joint attention," the ability to use one's attention to understand what others are thinking about and share that experience.

FEEDBACK, ASSESSMENT, AND PRACTICE

Follow up by observing game play and providing feedback to players about the types of thoughts they appear to be having and the types of thoughts others appear to be having, increasing student awareness of their own and others' thoughts.

During repeated play, use a "think aloud" process to attune students to what they and other students are thinking. Important think-aloud statements include the following:

- Do I want this card or not?

- It doesn't match any of my cards, so I don't want it. I will pass it to the next player.

(Continued)

(Continued)

- This card matches one of my cards, so I will keep it and choose a different card from my hand to discard.

- I better keep an eye on that pile of spoons in case someone else gets four of a kind before me and takes a spoon. That would mean I should take a spoon too, even if I don't get four of a kind.

TEACHING FOR GENERALIZATION

Once students have practiced this game several times, they have emerging understanding of experience sharing. Use verbal prompts in other school or home-based situations to help students describe the experiences they are sharing with others—for example, "Notice as I read this story aloud that you are all sharing the same experience of the same story but you may have different thoughts and feelings about the story."

Lesson 5: Suspicion

SUSPICION

Playing the part of "jewel thieves," students take on different identities, using observation and deductive reasoning to score points.

OBJECTIVES

Students will practice perspective-taking by seeing a situation from the perspective of a game "character" and answering questions from that perspective.

WHAT DOES THE RESEARCH SAY?

In this game, students use perspective-taking and complex reasoning skills to determine the "identities" of the other players. Developing these skills is shown to positively affect deep reading comprehension (LaRusso et al., 2016).

MATERIALS

- Suspicion board game (Wonder Forge)

Photo by Tracy Erdelyi. Used with permission.

Figure 6.3   This game is all about paying attention to point of view.

(Continued)

(Continued)

DIRECTIONS (FOR TWO TO SIX PLAYERS)

The directions included in the board game work well for the purposes of meeting the objective in this lesson. Give special attention to explaining how students answer the specific question "Can you see ____ ?" to identify that, in this case, "you" does not refer to the player but rather the game character that has been assigned to that player. It is also important to make sure players understand that from their characters' perspectives, they can always "see" themselves.

TALK ABOUT IT

This game requires students to think about what the game characters can "see" and to determine whether the character can see another specified character at a given time. Ask students if they were able to "put" themselves in their character's shoes. Was it ever confusing to think about what they could actually see versus thinking about only what their character could see?

FEEDBACK, ASSESSMENT, AND PRACTICE

Teachers can observe student performance throughout game play and determine whether students are accurately giving information about what a designated character can see. If accurate, game play is successful, if inaccurate, the teacher can offer reminders using the visual support of the character card to prompt the student to think about what the character can see.

TEACHING FOR GENERALIZATION

Try other games such as Ball Toss Communication (pp. 79–80) and Guess My Gaze (pp. 118–119) to provide practice seeing what others can see in new locations and situations.

Lesson 6: Picture Sequencing Activity

PICTURE SEQUENCING ACTIVITY

"What is this person doing [thinking, saying] and why?" Photographs that include people provide opportunities to teach and practice perspective-taking.

OBJECTIVES

Students will increase perspective-taking skills by sorting "static" photographs depicting a social scenario and interpreting what the people in the photographs might be doing, thinking, and saying.

WHAT DOES THE RESEARCH SAY?

In this activity, students interpret the clues in pictures that identify a specific location (a doctor's office for example), the people who are in that location, and the actions they might carry out in that location. They then negotiate with each other to determine the order in which to sequence the cards. Galinsky, Maddux, Gilin, and White (2008) describe the benefits of perspective-taking skills on negotiation—important in nearly every aspect of daily life.

MATERIALS

- Sequencing: Social Situations (Color Cards; these are six- to eight-step picture sequencing cards)

DIRECTIONS (FOR GROUPS OF SIX TO EIGHT STUDENTS; OR ADAPT THE DIRECTIONS HERE FOR USE WITH INDIVIDUAL STUDENTS)

1. Give a group of students a stack of cards to sort.

2. Explain: "These photos are all mixed up. Please look at the photos and place them in order based on what you think is happening in the pictures."

3. Have the students work together to sequence the cards, discussing what they think is happening in each picture. Provide help or prompting to ensure the cards are sequenced correctly.

4. Once the cards are sequenced, say, "Now I want you to think about how you would tell the story of what is happening in the pictures. Once you have thought of your story, please think of a title for your story."

(Continued)

(Continued)

5. Have students work together to narrate what is happening in the picture sequence and decide on a title.

6. Invite each group to tell their story aloud in a "frame by frame" format and then share the title of the story after listeners have had a chance to think in their own minds what the title might be.

7. Ask students to identify "clues" in the pictures that told them where the people in the photographs were, what they were doing, and why the title makes sense.

TALK ABOUT IT

This activity requires students to use their knowledge of social contexts. Expand on the activity by talking with students about how the way we are expected to say and do things may change depending on where we are. For example, ask students to think about what they know about restaurants (or cafes, coffee shops, etc.). What would they expect to see in a restaurant (e.g., people seated at tables)? What kind of communication do people use in a restaurant (e.g., when ordering food versus when visiting with friends or family)? What kinds of emotions might they expect to see (e.g., happiness, if people are having a good time)?

FEEDBACK, ASSESSMENT, AND PRACTICE

Observation of student performance during this activity is one way to evaluate student knowledge about the rules of a given social scenario. Provide instruction and practice for social understanding deficits or gaps in knowledge. If needed, collect data by category to identify if students are accurately interpreting the following:

- Thoughts

- Emotions

- Hidden curriculum (the unspoken rules of a given social scenario)

TEACHING FOR GENERALIZATION

One terrific way to teach for generalization in this activity is to follow the picture sort with a role-play. For example, say, "Now pretend you are the people in these photographs and carry out the story you have just told." Students can role-play what the different people in the photographs are thinking, feeling, and saying to each other. There are no words on these photographs, so student-generated language demonstrates their understanding of the social context and the thoughts and feelings of others.

Additionally, ask students to take the story into the next chapter. "Now let's pretend that the people in these pictures have decided to go to [the movies, the mall, a football game, a park, etc.] together. Make up a story and role-play the experience they have in the new situation."

Lesson 7: Faceland

FACELAND

With its amusement park theme and game-like format, this software features 1,000 real faces to help students learn to recognize facial expressions and corresponding emotions.

OBJECTIVES

Students will identify and differentiate the six universal emotions (happiness, sadness, anger, fear, disgust, surprise) and then practice making and recognizing the facial expressions that typically accompany those emotions. Students will identify situations that may cause a person to feel specific emotions.

WHAT DOES THE RESEARCH SAY?

In this activity, students interpret facial expressions and identify emotions. These skills not only provide the necessary foundation for higher level perspective-taking but also improve communication skills (Ekman, 2007).

MATERIALS

- Faceland (software program; Do2Learn)

DIRECTIONS (FOR INDIVIDUALS)

Use the directions included with the Faceland software. Students attend a "school" (watch a tutorial and answer questions) for each of the six universal emotions. Once each school lesson is complete, there is a corresponding game that, while fun and engaging, tests students' knowledge about that emotion.

Note: *The material in the games is presented in an "errorless learning" format, meaning that if the student chooses an incorrect answer, the correct one is provided. In addition, the tasks presented in the games move across the screen in varying ways, allowing a limited time for students to answer. This is important, as it aligns with research that suggests that perspective-taking must include instruction that occurs in a "real-time" format (Klin, Jones, Schultz, & Volkmar, 2003).*

TALK ABOUT IT

This game uses static pictures and video clips to provide explicit instruction about emotions—how to interpret facial expressions, how to make facial expressions, and how to understand the context in which

(Continued)

(Continued)

those corresponding emotions may occur. As students finish each school, connect the various scenarios in the lesson to students' own experiences. For example, after the school for "surprise" (which includes a surprise party theme), ask, "Have you ever been to a surprise party? Did you feel surprised? Did someone else feel surprised?"

FEEDBACK, ASSESSMENT, AND PRACTICE

Assessment is built into this software. When students sign in before completing the games and tutorials, the software tracks the student's responses and provides data about performance. After signing in, students must complete the game in sequence, with each game opening only after the related tutorial has been completed. The game also includes a "demo" mode that allows players to complete any tutorial or game in any order. Data on performance are not collected in demo mode.

TEACHING FOR GENERALIZATION

In Faceland, each of the six universal emotions is concretely "defined" by diagrams of faces that provide descriptions of visual clues. For example, surprise is defined as "eyebrows raised—curved and high," along with captions that describe the eyes and mouth of someone whose face shows surprise. As students complete the tutorials, encourage them to attend to the corresponding facial expressions that they observe throughout the day in a variety of contexts. Note that it is important to have students identify not only the facial expression but the context in which that emotion is occurring. Ask them, for example, to notice surprise by observing raised eyebrows, and so on.

Lesson 8: Listen, Care, Change

LISTEN, CARE, CHANGE

This activity takes a proactive approach to teaching students how to connect what they say and do to how others respond and what they, in turn, think and feel themselves.

OBJECTIVES

Students will increase their understanding of others' thoughts and feelings.

Students will increase their understanding of how thoughts and feelings motivate people's actions.

Listen, Care, Change			
I Say/I Do	Others Think/Feel	Others Say/Do	I Think/Feel
Throw a book in class	Scared	Leave Throw a book back Say, "knock it off"	Sad Scared Angry
Stay calm Take a breath Count to 5	Calm Comfortable	Carry on Be friendly	Happy Calm

Figure 6.4   **The first row shows the process of working through the results of a specific action. The second row shows the process of thinking through an alternative action that may lead to a more positive outcome.**

WHAT DOES THE RESEARCH SAY?

"Care" in the Listen, Care, Change activity means increasing empathy (understanding others' thoughts and feelings and caring about them). Empathy not only contributes to prosocial behavior but also contributes to the inhibition of aggressive and antisocial behavior (Eisenberg, Wilkens, & Di Giunta, 2010).

MATERIALS

- Paper

- Pencils

- Suggestion box (for students to place suggestions in; see Directions)

- Listen, Care, Change chart (Figure 6.5 blank template in Resources; see p. 134)

(Continued)

(Continued)

DIRECTIONS (FOR INDIVIDUALS, SMALL GROUP, OR WHOLE CLASS)

Note: *In advance of the lesson, make a Listen, Care, Change suggestion box. This can be as simple as a shoe box, oatmeal tub, or other suitable container with an opening cut in the lid so students can deposit their suggestions.*

1. Ask students to observe behaviors they see happening at school. Have them pay attention to words or actions that make them feel certain ways, such uncomfortable, annoyed, frustrated, sad, happy, supported, appreciated, and so on.

2. Have students make a note about these words and actions on a slip of paper and place it in the Listen, Care, Change suggestion box.

3. Designate a routine day/time to draw from the suggestion box and "Listen, Care, Change." Draw a slip from the box and read it silently first to determine if the words or actions are appropriate to process with the group in that moment. If not, make another selection or two to choose the best suggestion to process at that time.

4. Display the Listen, Care, Change chart provided in this book (enlarging it so students can easily read it or copying it on a whiteboard, chalkboard, or poster board). Then use the following process to complete the chart with students:

   a. **Column 1:** Write the selected words and/or actions from the suggestion box in column 1, along with a note about the context (relevant location and presence of others)—for example, "in class during math" or "on the playground at recess."

   b. **Column 2:** Ask students to offer suggestions for column 2, "Others Think/Feel." As students identify thoughts and feelings related to the words and actions in column 1, record them in column 2.

   c. **Column 3:** Ask students to identify what people are likely to say or do when they have thoughts and feelings, such as those listed in column 2. It is important to note that the words and actions in this step relate specifically to the thoughts and feelings that have been identified (in column 2)—NOT necessarily the words and/or actions in column 1. In other words, the words and actions identified for column 3 may or may not be identical to what happened when the student originally observed the behavior. Write the words and actions that relate to the identified thoughts and feelings in column 3.

   d. **Column 4:** Ask students, "When people say these words or do these actions (column 3) what do you think? How do you feel?" Record responses in column 4, then ask: "Are these thoughts and feelings that you enjoy having or would like to have again?" (These responses are not recorded.)

5. Draw an arrow from column 4 back to column 1 (as in the sample chart). Guide students in connecting the resulting thoughts and feelings (column 4) with the original words and actions (column 1). See Teaching for Generalization for a follow-up activity that provides practice with thinking through opposing words and actions for a different outcome.

TALK ABOUT IT

This activity is useful for helping students connect their words and actions to resulting thoughts and feelings. They can then determine whether those resulting thoughts and feelings are ones that they want to have again and again. "Keeping my body calm during morning meeting" and "happy and comfortable" are just a couple of examples that often come up when using this activity with students.

The "context" portion of column 1 is very important, as the rules that govern our social interactions change depending on context. For example, sudden, fast movements may be expected behaviors on the soccer field but not in the school cafeteria. Have students talk about how the actions and words they use may change depending on the place and situation. Ask them to list situations in which sudden, speedy movements may be better and situations where slower, less abrupt movements might be best.

Please note that while the language on the chart includes "I" and "others," specific people are not identified on this chart. Students can complete the social learning related to challenging or awkward behaviors with anonymity in the larger group context. Talk with students about putting themselves in someone else's place, so they can do the perspective-taking needed to imagine how they might feel if they had been the person who said or did something listed in column 1.

FEEDBACK, ASSESSMENT, AND PRACTICE

With this activity, it is frequently necessary to help students with accurately generating how others think and feel. As students become more independent with accurately predicting others' thoughts and feelings, they demonstrate an increase in their perspective-taking abilities.

TEACHING FOR GENERALIZATION

Take the learning in Listen, Care, Change further by following the initial process with a row that charts an opposing behavior. The sample chart in this lesson shows one example of how this works. As another example, let's say the note from the suggestion box is "blurting out answers in class during math instruction." After completing the chart for "I Say/I Do" (Steps 4–5), complete row 2 for an "opposing" behavior. In the case of blurting out answers, an opposing action might be "raising my hand and waiting to be called on in class during math."

Students can further generalize their learning by predicting other words and actions that occur either during the school day or at home and in the community. Introduce students to the vocabulary and concepts of Predict, Care, Change. Ask about times when they might be able to predict how others will feel when experiencing specific words and actions.

Lesson 9: Guess My Gaze

GUESS MY GAZE

Students learn that eye gaze offers clues to what people are thinking.

OBJECTIVES

Students will increase their ability to follow another person's eye gaze and their ability to interpret another person's thoughts by following eye gaze. They will also use eye gaze themselves as a form of nonverbal communication to show another person what they are thinking about.

WHAT DOES THE RESEARCH SAY?

Following eye gaze is one way that people can guess what others are thinking about. In this activity, students follow eye gaze to receive information. A person's eye gaze gives information about intentions and future actions. Interpreting eye gaze engages social cognitive processes such as theory of mind (Clifford & Palmer, 2018). When parents and teachers want children to know where to look, for example, the adults often look at the location themselves as a means of sharing what they are thinking about. This activity helps children "tune-in" to the meanings that accompany eye gaze.

MATERIALS

No materials needed

DIRECTIONS (FOR INDIVIDUALS, SMALL GROUP, OR WHOLE CLASS)

1. Explain that people "give away their thinking" with their eyes. In other words, "The things people look at give you a clue about what they are thinking about."

2. Share with students that they are going to practice using a person's eyes to guess what that person is thinking. Start with a warm-up:

   a. Begin by looking at a student (A). Ask another student (B), "Who am I looking at?"

   b. When Student B replies with the name of Student A, continue looking at Student A and say, "Right! Now, who do you think I am thinking about?"

   c. Student B repeats Student A's name.

3. Respond, saying, "Right! Now, I am going to look somewhere else. See if you can guess what I am looking at."

   a. Select any object with a purpose—for example, the teacher's computer—and look at it.

   b. Students guess, "your computer."

   c. Reply, "Right! What do you think I am thinking about?"

   d. Students guess.

4. Provide feedback and guidance based on students' guesses. For example, prompt a student who repeats "your computer," by saying, "Yes, I am looking at my computer, but what might I be thinking about?" Correct guesses might include, "Your work," "Your email," and so on.

5. Once students understand the process, they can take turns leading Guess My Gaze to practice using eye gaze as a clue to what they are thinking about.

TALK ABOUT IT

Ask students if they notice that following eye gaze becomes more challenging as the distance between the eyes and the object increases. Discuss times when the teacher (or leader) may need to be close to the person or object that is the subject of Guess My Gaze. As a general rule, students may need to start with shorter distances to ensure success. Talk with students about creative things they might do to ensure success if they notice someone is having difficulty following their gaze. In addition to getting closer to the object, they might need to add pointing with their finger or even using an electronic pointer or flashlight to reveal the answer.

FEEDBACK, ASSESSMENT, AND PRACTICE

The most important feedback for teachers to give students in this activity is that eye gaze is a "clue." In revealing the object that a person is thinking about, the student needs to then think about what functions that object might serve to the person who is looking at it. For example, a person checking the clock is likely not thinking, "This is a clock," but more likely thinking, "How much time before lunch," or "How much time do I have to finish?"

Once students have this feedback and understanding, assess by observation for the accuracy of their perspective-taking skills. Practice should include students following teacher eye gaze, the teacher following student eye gaze, and students following each other's eye gaze.

TEACHING FOR GENERALIZATION

Once introduced, Guess My Gaze is an easy activity to repeat throughout the day at any time. Simply prompt, "Guess my gaze," "Follow my eyes," or "I am showing you what I am thinking about with my eyes" to engage students in the activity in a variety of locations and situations. Build practice into everyday activities—for example, "I am going to choose the next student to ___ with my eyes." Prompt students to use their eyes to choose partners for teamwork or to "ask" for something they want, such as a book they can't reach.

Lesson 10: Bubble Talk

BUBBLE TALK

This photo-caption game actively engages players in trying to detect what a person (or animal) in a photograph might be thinking.

OBJECTIVES

Students will improve their perspective-taking skills by interpreting what a person or animal in a picture would say in a given situation.

WHAT DOES THE RESEARCH SAY?

Diverse teams perform more creatively when the team members are instructed to take each other's perspective (Hoever, Van Knippenberg, Van Ginkel, & Barkema, 2012). In this game, students use creativity and perspective-taking, skills that will positively impact peer relationships and academic performance.

MATERIALS

- Bubble Talk board game (University Games)

DIRECTIONS (FOR THREE TO EIGHT PLAYERS)

Follow the directions included with this game as written. Students provide captions for pictures that show people or animals with "thinking bubbles." Similar to Apples to Apples, students take turns judging which caption appeals to their own thoughts about the picture.

TALK ABOUT IT

Tell students that anytime they are making a guess about what someone else is thinking they are using perspective-taking skills. Ask them to notice the number of different captions that are used for a single picture in the game. The differences represent their differing perspectives. Emphasize that the different captions show that when two people share the same experience (in this case, looking at a photograph), they can have different thoughts and feelings about that experience.

FEEDBACK, ASSESSMENT, AND PRACTICE

Game instructions include four variations on the original instructions. Use these variations for practice and for further teaching. The fourth variation requires the player who is the "judge" to not only select the best caption for a picture but to also guess which other player played that card. This requires perspective-taking in two ways: understanding what the person or animal pictured may be thinking and understanding the thinking of all of the other players to make an accurate guess about what another player might say or do.

TEACHING FOR GENERALIZATION

Generalize the perspective-taking skills applied in this game by having students predict the thoughts of people or animals in pictures in other places—for example, children's books, magazines, or video clips. The Bubble Talk game supplies captions and includes a variation for students to generate their own captions. While the game captions are humorous, the teaching for generalization can include more serious examples, answering the question, "What would a person say in this situation?" The most sophisticated generalization of this skill is the ability to predict another person's thoughts or words in real-time, real-life experiences.

Conclusion

One of my graduate students, an experienced fourth-grade teacher, decided to apply some of her new knowledge about social emotional teaching in her classroom. She wanted to teach a lesson about (not) "blurting out the answer." She gave some thought to the problem. Blurting is noisy in the classroom, but that is not really the problem. When the same few students blurt out answers, always wanting to give the answer first, the teacher has no way to assess the progress and knowledge of quieter students.

This teacher applied the Listen, Care, Change strategy (see p. 97) to explicitly teach the whole class that she must think about all of their answers during math, and that when a few students blurt out answers, she can't hear the answers from other students. The students were actively engaged in the lesson, collaboratively thinking about their words and actions, the impact on others, and how they can change. Once finished the group had an "aha" moment, recognizing that blurting might be a fast way to show knowledge of the answer, but it does not help the teacher achieve the goal of understanding what each student knows. The very next day, during math instruction, hands were raised, and students waited before answering. This teacher reported back to me about the effectiveness of her direct instruction with the group, saying, "I don't know why I haven't been doing this for the last ten years!" She was amazed at how easily a 10-minute lesson in social emotional learning instantly changed a frustrating, recurring classroom problem.

Not every effort of social teaching will pay off so quickly, but the work will positively impact students in a way that not only improves their academic achievements but also enriches their communication skills and relationships. Teachers will deepen their understanding of the nuances and complexities of social emotional learning with every lesson they teach.

Figure I.1 Reaction Energy Cycles Visual 1

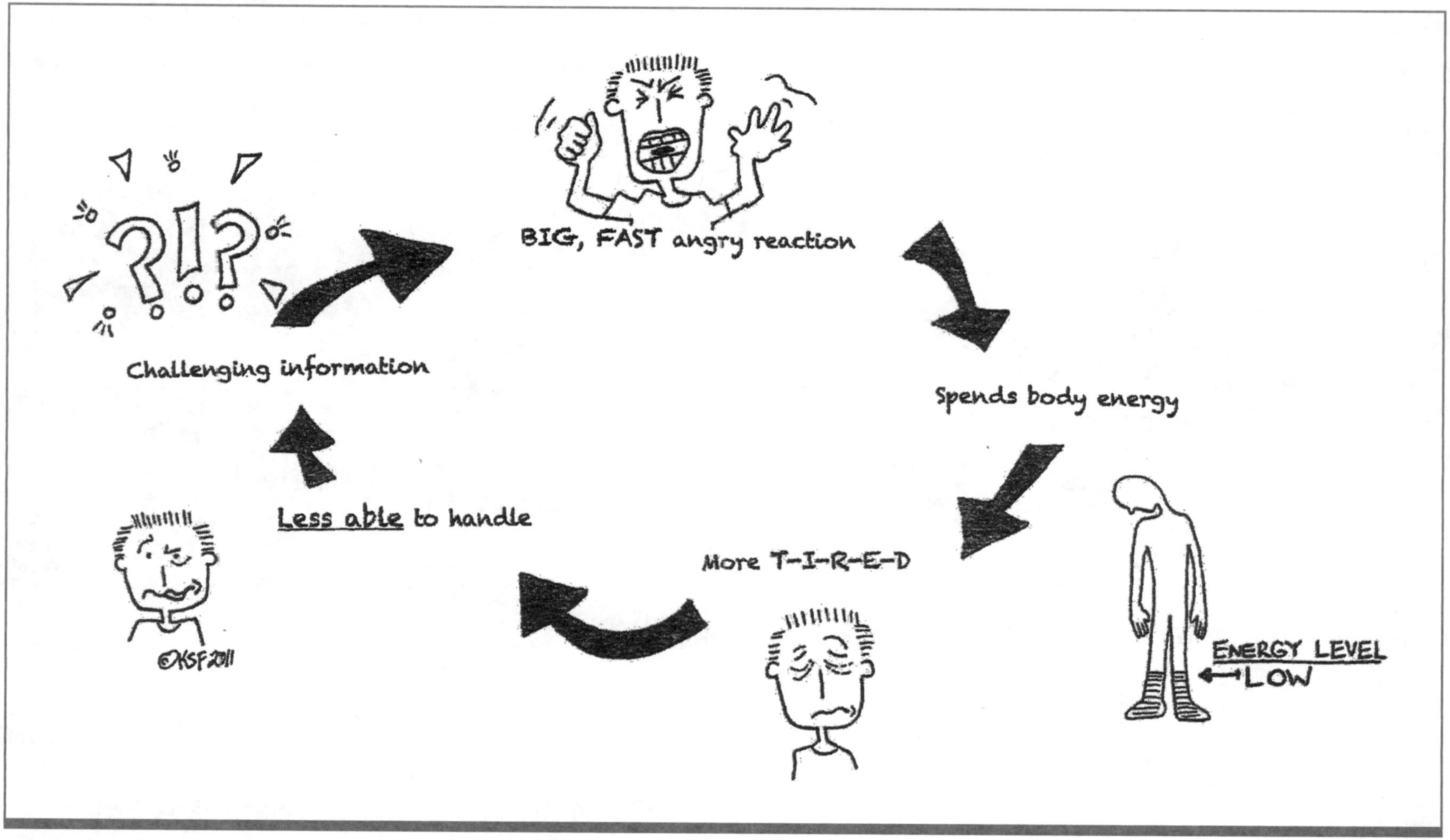
?!?
BIG, FAST angry reaction
Spends body energy
ENERGY LEVEL
LOW
More T-I-R-E-D
Less able to handle
Challenging information
©KSF2011

Created by Kathleen Fechter. Used with permission.

Figure I.2   Reaction Energy Cycles Visual 2

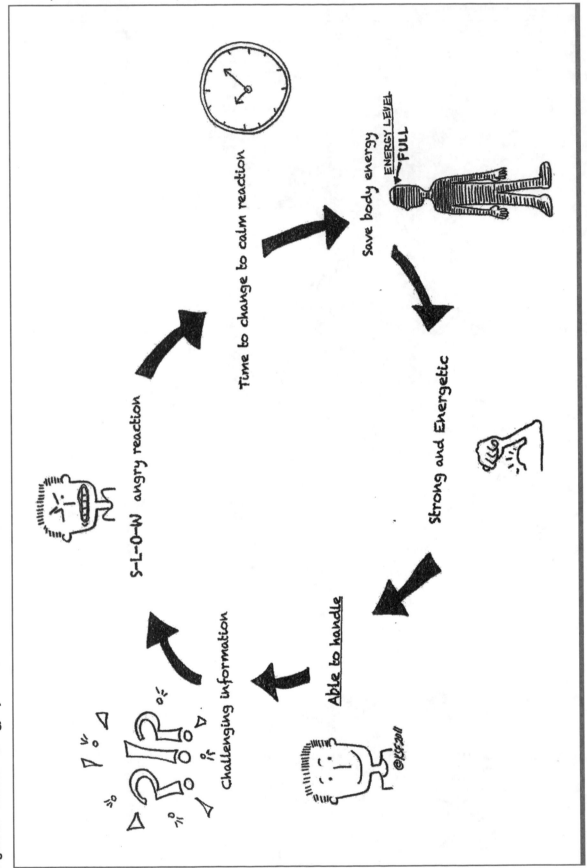

Figure 2.4   Chill Out Game Cards

I can take 3 deep breaths before saying/doing anything else.	Keep trying!
Accept and move on.	I can just wait. I can handle this problem in a little while.
I can defeat this problem without crying.	I can tense up and relax my muscles to help my body feel calm.
This moment will pass.	I need some help, please.

(Continued)

Chill Out Game Cards, Continued

Even hard work is easier with a calm brain.

I know this is a tiny problem.

I feel better if I stay calmer.

I CAN do this.

My parents, my teacher, or my friends will help me if I ask.

Positive thoughts = good choices

Figure 2.7   Flexibility Points Visual

Flexibility Points

You will get a flexibility point in group for every time you use the **"ACCEPT AND MOVE ON"** strategy.

ACCEPT AND MOVE ON:

1. Feel disappointed or frustrated.

2. Say:

3. Move on.

1 point!
➔ Important note: NO partial points available.
➔ Steps 1, 2, and 3 MUST be combined to earn the point.

Figure 4.2   Follow-Up Questions Visual

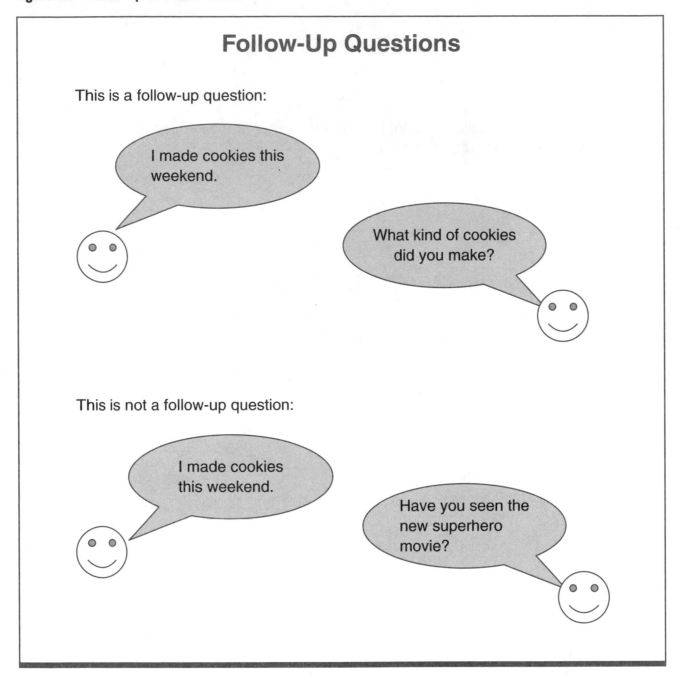

Figure 4.7 Relationship Types Cards

AUTHORITY	COMMUNALITY	RECIPROCITY
I SAY/YOU DO	SHARE AND SHARE ALIKE	GIVE AND TAKE/GIVE AND GET
Parent/Child	Close Friends	Waitstaff/Patron
Teacher/Student	Significant Other	Store Clerk/Customer

(Continued)

Police Officer/Citizen	Spouse	Classmates
Airline Attendant/Passenger	Siblings	Coworkers
Boss/Employee	Boyfriend/Girlfriend	Acquaintances

Figure 4.8 Mixing Ideas Mission Visual

Mixing Ideas Mission

Use the steps for mixing ideas in your everyday life at home and at school. The steps are the following:

1. SAY your idea or plan. Examples:

    * My idea is _____.

    * I want to _____.

    * How about if we _____?

2. ASK the other person (or people), "What do you think?" Then LISTEN and THINK about the other person's answer.

3. MIX the two ideas together.

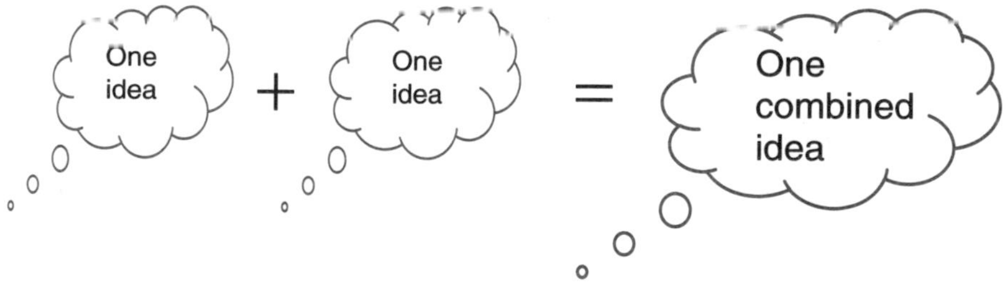

When you get caught by your teacher or parent mixing ideas together, you get two things:

1. Mixing idea <u>points</u> to bring back to group

2. A <u>reputation</u> with your friends and family that you are considerate, flexible, and easy to work with

Figure 6.5   Listen, Care, Change Chart

Listen, Care, Change			
I Say/I Do	**Others Think/Feel**	**Others Say/Do**	**I Think/Feel**

References

Aizikovitsh-Udi, E., & Cheng, D. (2015). Developing critical thinking skills from dispositions to abilities: Mathematics education from early childhood to high school. *Creative Education, 6*, 455–462. https://doi.org/10.4236/ce.2015.64045

An, J. E., Lee, H. B., & Kwon, Y. H. (2019). Effects of collaborative activities using picture books on self-regulation and perspective-taking abilities of young children. *Korean Journal of Childcare and Education, 15*(3), 61–81. https://doi.org/10.14698/jkcce.2019.15.03.061

Baio, J., Wiggins, L., Christensen, D. L., Maenner, M. J., Daniels, J., Warren, Z., . . . Durkin, M. S. (2018). Prevalence of autism spectrum disorder among children aged 8 years—autism and developmental disabilities monitoring network, 11 sites, United States, 2014. *MMWR Surveillance Summaries, 67*(6), 1. https://doi.org/10.15585/mmwr.ss6706a1

Bandura, A. (1986). *Social foundations of thought and action: A social cognitive theory.* Englewood Cliffs, NJ: Prentice-Hall.

Bandura, A. (1989). Human agency in social cognitive theory. *The American Psychologist, 44*, 1175–1184. https://doi.org/10.1037/0003-066X.44.9.1175

Baron-Cohen, S. (2000). Theory of mind and autism: A fifteen year review. *Understanding Other Minds: Perspectives From Developmental Cognitive Neuroscience, 2*, 3–20.

Baron-Cohen, S., O'Riordan, M., Jones, R., Stone, V. E., & Plaisted, K. (1999). A new test of social sensitivity: Detection of faux pas in normal children and children with Asperger syndrome. *Journal of Autism and Developmental Disorders, 29*, 407–418.

Bosacki, S., & Astington, J. W. (1999). Theory of mind in preadolescence: Relations between social understanding and social competence. *Social Development, 8*(2), 237–255. https://doi.org/10.1111/1467-9507.00093

Brooks, A. W., & John, L. K. (2018). The surprising power of questions. *Harvard Business Review, 96*(3), 60–67.

Buron, K., & Curtis, M. B. (2012). *The incredible 5-point scale: Assisting students in understanding social interactions and controlling their emotional responses.* Shawnee Mission, KS: AAPC Publishing.

Clifford, C. W., & Palmer, C. J. (2018). Adaptation to the direction of others' gaze: A review. *Frontiers in Psychology, 9*, 2165. https://doi.org/10.3389/fpsyg.2018.02165

Diamond, A. (2013). Executive functions. *Annual Review of Psychology, 64*, 135–168. https://doi.org/10.1146/annurev-psych-113011-143750

Diamond, A., & Lee, K. (2011). Interventions shown to aid executive function development in children 4 to 12 years old. *Science, 333*(6045), 959–964. https://doi.org/10.1126/science.1204529

Duckworth, A. L., & Steinberg, L. (2015). Unpacking self-control. *Child Development Perspectives, 9*(1), 32–37. https://doi.org/10.1111/cdep.12107

Dunn, W. (1999). *Sensory profile* (Vol. 555). San Antonio, TX: Psychological Corporation.

Durand, M. V., & Crimmins, D. B. (1992). *The motivation assessment scale* (MAS) *administration guide.* Topeka, KS: Monaco & Associates Incorporated.

Durlak, J. A., Weissberg, R. P., Dymnicki, A. B., Taylor, R. D., & Schellinger, K. B. (2011). The impact of enhancing students' social and emotional learning: A meta-analysis of school-based universal interventions. *Child Development, 82*(1), 405–432. https://doi.org/10.1111/j.1467-8624.2010.01564.x

Eaves, M., & Leathers, D. G. (2017). *Successful nonverbal communication: Principles and applications.* Abingdon, UK: Routledge. https://doi.org/10.4324/9781315542317

Eisenberg, N., Michalik, N., Spinrad, T. L., Hofer, C., Kupfer, A., Valiente, C., . . . Reiser, M. (2007). The relations of effortful control and impulsivity to children's sympathy: A longitudinal study. *Cognitive Development, 22*(4), 544–567. https://doi.org/10.1016/j.cogdev.2007.08.003

Eisenberg, N., Wilkens, N., & Di Giunta, L. (2010). Empathy-related responding: Associations with prosocial behavior, aggression, and intergroup relations. *Social Issues and Policy Review, 4*(1), 143–180.

Ekman, P. (2007). *Emotions revealed: Recognizing faces and feelings to improve communication and emotional life.* New York, NY: Macmillan.

Faggella-Luby, M. N., Graner, P. S., Deshler, D. D., & Drew, S. V. (2012). Building a house on sand: Why disciplinary literacy is not sufficient to replace general strategies for adolescent learners who struggle. *Topics in Language Disorders, 32*(1), 69–84. https://doi.org/10.1097/TLD.0b013e318245618e

Fiske, A. P. (1992). The four elementary forms of sociality: Framework for a unified theory of social relations. *Psychological Review, 99,* 689–723.

Galinsky, A. D., Maddux, W. W., Gilin, D., & White, J. B. (2008). Why it pays to get inside the head of your opponent: The differential effects of perspective taking and empathy in negotiations. *Psychological Science, 19*(4), 378–384. https://doi.org/10.1111/j.1467-9280.2008.02096.x

Gehlbach, H., Marietta, G., King, A. M., Karutz, C., Bailenson, J. N., & Dede, C. (2015). Many ways to walk a mile in another's moccasins: Type of social perspective taking and its effect on negotiation outcomes. *Computers in Human Behavior, 52,* 523–532. https://doi.org/10.1016/j.chb.2014.12.035

Ghertner, R., & Groves, L. (2018). The opioid crisis and economic opportunity: Geographic and economic trends (ASPE Research Brief), 1–22.

Grant, A. M., & Berry, J. W. (2011). The necessity of others is the mother of invention: Intrinsic and prosocial motivations, perspective taking, and creativity. *Academy of Management Journal, 54*(1), 73–96.

Gray, C. (1994). *Comic strip conversations: Illustrated interactions that teach conversation skills to students with autism and related disorders.* Arlington, TX: Future Horizons.

Gray, C. (2015). *The new social story book.* Arlington, TX: Future Horizons.

Heider, F., & Simmel, M. (1944). An experimental study of apparent behavior. *The American Journal of Psychology, 57*(2), 243–259. https://doi.org/ 10.2307/1416950

Hieneman, M. (2015). Positive behavior support for individuals with behavior challenges. *Behavior Analysis in Practice, 8*(1), 101–108. https://doi.org/10.1007/s40617-015-0051-6

Hoever, I. J., Van Knippenberg, D., Van Ginkel, W. P., & Barkema, H. G. (2012). Fostering team creativity: Perspective taking as key to unlocking diversity's potential. *Journal of Applied Psychology, 97*(5), 982–996.

Hofmann, W., Schmeichel, B. J., & Baddeley, A. D. (2012). Executive functions and self-regulation. *Trends in Cognitive Sciences, 16*(3), 174–180. https://doi.org/10.1016/j.tics.2012.01.006

Horner, R. H., Sugai, G., & Anderson, C. M. (2010). Examining the evidence base for school-wide positive behavior support. *Focus on Exceptional Children, 42*(8).

Hutchins, T. L., & Prelock, P. A. (2016). *The theory of mind atlas.* (Unpublished manuscript). Available at theoryofmindinventory.com

Johnson, S. B., Riis, J. L., & Noble, K. G. (2016). State of the art review: Poverty and the developing brain. *Pediatrics, 137*(4), e20153075.

Jones, S. N., & Kahn, J. (2017). *The evidence base for how we learn: Supporting students' social, emotional, and academic development.* Washington, DC: The Aspen Institute.

Karably, K., & Zabrucky, K. M. (2017). Children's metamemory: A review of the literature and implications for the classroom. *International Electronic Journal of Elementary Education, 2*(1), 32–52.

Klin, A., Jones, W., Schultz, R., & Volkmar, F. (2003). The enactive mind, or from actions to cognition: Lessons from autism. *Philosophical Transactions of the Royal Society of London. Series B: Biological Sciences, 358*(1430), 345–360. https://doi.org/10.1098/rstb.2002.1202

Koffka, K. (2013). *Principles of Gestalt Psychology.* New York, NY: Routledge.

Koziol, L. F., & Lutz, J. T. (2013). From movement to thought: The development of executive function. *Applied Neuropsychology: Child, 2*(2), 104–115. https://doi.org/10.1080/21622965.2013.748386

LaRusso, M., Kim, H. Y., Selman, R., Uccelli, P., Dawson, T., Jones, S., . . . Snow, C. (2016). Contributions of academic language, perspective taking, and complex reasoning to deep reading comprehension. *Journal of Research on Educational Effectiveness, 9*(2), 201–222. https://doi.org/10.1080/19345747.2015.1116035

Lissak, G. (2018). Adverse physiological and psychological effects of screen time on children and adolescents: Literature review and case study. *Environmental Research, 164,* 149–157. https://doi.org/10.1016/j.envres.2018.01.015

McAfee, J. (2013). *Navigating the social world: A curriculum for individuals with Asperger's syndrome, high functioning autism and related disorders.* Arlington, TX: Future Horizons.

Mehrabian, A., & Ferris, S. R. (1967). Inference of attitudes from nonverbal communication in two channels. *Journal of Consulting Psychology, 31*(3), 248. http://dx.doi.org/10.1037/h0024648

Mehrabian, A., & Wiener, M. (1967). Decoding of inconsistent communications. *Journal of Personality and Social Psychology, 6*(1), 109. http://dx.doi.org/10.1037/h0024532

Myles, B. S., Trautman, M. L., & Schelvan, R. L. (2004). *The hidden curriculum: Practical solutions for understanding unstated rules in social situations*. Shawnee KS: AAPC Publishing.

Navarro, J., & Karlins, M. (2008). *What every body is saying*. New York, NY: HarperCollins.

Neck, C. P., & Manz, C. C. (1992). Thought self-leadership: The influence of self-talk and mental imagery on performance. *Journal of Organizational Behavior, 13*(7), 681–699. https://doi.org/10.1002/job.4030130705

Nigg, J. T. (2017). Annual research review: On the relations among self-regulation, self-control, executive functioning, effortful control, cognitive control, impulsivity, risk-taking, and inhibition for developmental psychopathology. *Journal of Child Psychology and Psychiatry, 58*(4), 361–383. https://doi.org/10.1111/jcpp.12675

Pedersen, T. (2018). Theory of mind. *Psych Central*. Retrieved on May 14, 2019, from https://psychcentral.com/encyclopedia/theory-of-mind/

Pinker, S. (2008). *The stuff of thought: Language as a window into human nature*. New York, NY: Penguin.

Repacholi, B., & Slaughter, V. (Eds.). (2004). *Individual differences in theory of mind: Implications for typical and atypical development*. New York, NY: Psychology Press.

Reyes, Z., Eusebio, E., Wagner, S., Du, F., Tan, A., Tannler, M., & Yoo, S. H. (2015). *Positive self-talk during conversations: A buffer against negative emotions*. Poster session presented at the 95th Annual Convention for the Western Psychological Association, Las Vegas, NV.

Shoda, Y., Mischel, W., & Peake, P. K. (1990). Predicting adolescent cognitive and self-regulatory competencies from preschool delay of gratification: Identifying diagnostic conditions. *Developmental Psychology, 26*(6), 978. https://doi.org/10.1037/0012-1649.26.6.978

Stiller, J., & Dunbar, R. I. (2007). Perspective-taking and memory capacity predict social network size. *Social Networks, 29*(1), 93–104. https://doi.org/10.1016/j.socnet.2006.04.001

Thiébaut, F. I., White, S. J., Walsh, A., Klargaard, S. K., Wu, H. C., Rees, G., & Burgess, P. W. (2016). Does faux pas detection in adult autism reflect differences in social cognition or decision-making abilities? *Journal of Autism and Developmental Disorders, 46*(1), 103–112.

Tran, V. D. (2014). The effects of cooperative learning on the academic achievement and knowledge retention. *International Journal of Higher Education, 3*(2), 131.

Tsukayama, E., Duckworth, A. L., & Kim, B. (2013). Domain-specific impulsivity in school-age children. *Developmental Science, 16*(6), 879–893. https://doi.org/10.1111/desc.12067

von Ravensberg, H., & Blakely, A. (2014). *When to use functional behavioral assessment? Best practice vs. legal guidance*. (Issue 18). Technical Assistance Center on Positive Behavioral Interventions and Supports. Retrieved from https://www.pbis.org/evaluation/evaluation-briefs/when-to-use-fba

Willis, K. (2016). *Can you wait? The effects of induced gratitude and pride on children's ability to delay gratification* (Doctoral dissertation). Retrieved from TCU Digital Repository.

Wimmer, H., & Perner, J. (1983). Beliefs about beliefs: Representation and constraining function of wrong beliefs in young children's understanding of deception. *Cognition, 13*(1), 103–128. https://doi.org/10.1016/0010-0277(83)90004-5

Index

A SAGE Publishing Company

Helping educators make the greatest impact

CORWIN HAS ONE MISSION: to enhance education through intentional professional learning.

We build long-term relationships with our authors, educators, clients, and associations who partner with us to develop and continuously improve the best evidence-based practices that establish and support lifelong learning.

Solutions YOU WANT | *Experts* YOU TRUST | *Results* YOU NEED

EVENTS

> > > **INSTITUTES**
>
> Corwin Institutes provide large regional events where educators collaborate with peers and learn from industry experts. Prepare to be recharged and motivated!
>
> **corwin.com/institutes**

ON-SITE PD

> > > **ON-SITE PROFESSIONAL LEARNING**
>
> Corwin on-site PD is delivered through high-energy keynotes, practical workshops, and custom coaching services designed to support knowledge development and implementation.
>
> **corwin.com/pd**

> > > **PROFESSIONAL DEVELOPMENT RESOURCE CENTER**
>
> The PD Resource Center provides school and district PD facilitators with the tools and resources needed to deliver effective PD.
>
> **corwin.com/pdrc**

ONLINE

> > > **ADVANCE**
>
> Designed for K–12 teachers, Advance offers a range of online learning options that can qualify for graduate-level credit and apply toward license renewal.
>
> **corwin.com/advance**

Contact a PD Advisor at (800) 831-6640 or visit www.corwin.com for more information